By the Waters of Paradise

By the Waters of Paradise

An American Story of Racism and Rupture in a Jewish Family

CLARE KINBERG

WAYNE STATE UNIVERSITY PRESS
DETROIT

ISBN 9780814352755 (paperback)
ISBN 9780814352762 (ebook)

Library of Congress Control Number: 2025932985

Cover design by Mindy Basinger Hill.

Publication of this book was made possible through the generosity of the Bertha M. and Hyman Herman Endowed Memorial Fund.

Wayne State University Press rests on Waawiyaataanong, also referred to as Detroit, the ancestral and contemporary homeland of the Three Fires Confederacy. These sovereign lands were granted by the Ojibwe, Odawa, Potawatomi, and Wyandot Nations, in 1807, through the Treaty of Detroit. Wayne State University Press affirms Indigenous sovereignty and honors all tribes with a connection to Detroit. With our Native neighbors, the press works to advance educational equity and promote a better future for the earth and all people.

Wayne State University Press
Leonard N. Simons Building
4809 Woodward Avenue
Detroit, Michigan 48201-1309

Visit us online at wsupress.wayne.edu.

The historian's task consists of establishing the organic connection between the separate links of the historical process.

—Simon Dubnow

CONTENTS

INTRODUCTION

The Shadows

For forty years, I tried to find my Aunt Rose, my father's sister. I hadn't known she existed until, as a young teen, I began to feel her presence as an occasional shadow in my family's life. My father's brother and sisters were the tall oaks in the little woods of my childhood. Our family (my parents, my four siblings, and I) and my father's extended Ashkenazi Jewish family (his siblings and their children and grandchildren) lived in connecting neighborhoods. We saw each other at least monthly at our rotating Sunday socials, during which we had dinner, and the women played canasta while the men played poker, and the kids dashed in and out of rooms. I grew up secure in the knowledge that the Kinbergs of St. Louis were a proud and loyal clan. I had no idea that one of the trees had been walled off into a separate garden.

When, at age twelve or so, I overheard my father preparing to take a short trip, I barely noted it as a curiosity. Dad was standing in the doorway to the kitchen of our split-level home in suburban St. Louis County. The light was behind him, and his face was in shadow. Even though I was looking at him, I didn't see him. My mother was behind him, and

I heard her say that Dad was going to Vandalia to see his sister Rose. This information was so unexpected and out of place that, like a jigsaw piece that obviously didn't fit into the puzzle I was just beginning to assemble, I put the information aside. I didn't even examine the possibility of another aunt for several years. I didn't ask any questions. With a child's blink, I filed away the knowledge that there was a Rose in Vandalia.

I came of age in a nuclear family of white-flight early adopters during the paradigm-shifting years of the Civil Rights Movement. When my father heard, in 1962, that a Black family had moved within a few blocks of our near-to-the-city suburb, he began the search for a new home as far west in the county as he could afford.

My father's family had been moving west, block by block, for two generations. The Kinbergs' St. Louis experience matched the well-worn American urban narrative of Jewish neighborhoods becoming Black neighborhoods when the Jews moved out. The related history of Jewish family-owned businesses staying in the old neighborhoods even after the Jews left also fit my family's story.

My father's sister Rose was an exception; her life did not follow this pattern. After she left St. Louis in the 1930s, she moved into a segregated Black neighborhood in another city with her African American husband and ended up living the rest of her life on the shore of a small lake in a rural Black community.

Aunt Rose and I grew up a generation apart among Ashkenazi Jews whom I had been raised to believe were completely segregated from African American families. But the separation was both a lie and a truth so deep it was invisible even as it was enforced. Despite Jim Crow and antimiscegenation laws, and despite racist social conventions, racial borders were commonly crossed.

Both Aunt Rose and I lived our adult lives with Black people. My wife is descended from enslaved Black women and their white owners, and our adopted daughters were born of Black women in the United States. For me, being in an interracial family has meant navigating persistent racial segregation and living intimately with the effects of racism on those closest to my heart.

Because of its impact on my daughters, I am conscious of how race operates in every interaction I have. Like a woman walking alone at night considers her safety, like a Jew reading the daily news with an eye to evidence of antisemitism, awareness of race and its implications for my family never leaves me. But I'm still learning what to do with my awareness of the dangers. As a woman, I've learned to clench keys in my fist, ready to deliver a powerful defensive punch. As a Jew, I've internalized the need to keep a bag packed, ready for the historically predicated need to escape.

Growing up in my birth family and my neighborhoods, I did not acquire the insight or tools to cope with anti-Black racism; rather, I learned how to perpetrate it. But for the racism of my family of origin, I might have grown up knowing Aunt Rose and knowing her husband's family as *machatunim* (Yiddish for the in-laws' family). If Aunt Rose had been part of our lives, part of my memories—the stories that shaped my future—I would have been grounded at a younger age in a deeper truth of how the caste system works in America.

• • •

My Aunt Rose died on my twenty-seventh birthday, February 6, 1982. I know that now because I found her death certificate on the internet in 2016, thirty-four years after she'd died. I was sixty-one.

In a flash, a doorway to Aunt Rose's life opened on my screen. She had resided less than two hours from where I lived in Michigan with my wife, Patti, and our two daughters.

Seeing Aunt Rose's death certificate, I felt a flood of regret that I hadn't found her while she was still alive. I became determined to find her burial place. I was awash with wonder at the coincidence of her closeness to me.

My search for Aunt Rose's life was made easier because she herself had provided the information on her death certificate. Though she didn't know—or remember—her mother's maiden name, she usefully included the name of the funeral home she intended to have take care of her body and the cemetery where she was to be buried. The funeral home still had a slim manila folder for her that contained an obituary from the *Cassopolis Vigilant*: "Born in St. Louis, Missouri, there are no known survivors at this time. Several close friends looked after the deceased during her illness." The obituary implied that her friends did not know whether she had family or how to contact them. Did she keep her birth family hidden from her friends, or did she ask her friends not to reveal her birth family? Reading "no known survivors *at this time*" confirmed that her separation had been permanent and created new possibilities and conundrums for me. Perhaps she'd anticipated that one day a niece would come looking for her.

Despite my long career as an editor of a Jewish feminist political and literary journal, when I stood on Aunt Rose's unmarked grave, I felt for the first time that I had to become a writer because I needed to tell her story.

The book I imagined told a story about Rose Kinberg alongside another story about her husband, Zebedee Arnwine. Their separate stories would merge for a while and then separate again. I wanted to tell a story of how a non-Jewish (my presumption) African American man and an Ashkenazi Jewish woman had tried to make a life together against and amid generations of genocidal racism and antisemitism. I wanted to record my search for my Aunt Rose's life and what I could find of the people she knew and the places she'd lived. By writing this story, I knew I would need to examine my own interracial family life, my Jewishness, my choices.

Before Aunt Rose and Mr. Arnwine met, they'd lived for more than twenty-five years in their separate communities—she with immigrant Jewish parents in St. Louis, and he in a family of Black farmers in Muskogee, Oklahoma. I've located records showing Mr. Arnwine had already been married three times and had three children—one with each of his wives—prior to his marriage with my Aunt Rose. Aunt Rose, too, had married young and had a child before divorcing. Sometime during the Great Depression, my Aunt Rose and Mr. Arnwine moved to Chicago together without their young children.

When Aunt Rose died in 1982, I had recently met Patti, the woman who would become my life partner. Patti and I both wanted children.

I have lived my life as a lesbian and feminist activist while being active in the Jewish community. I have moved many times: from St. Louis to the rural Ozarks, then to Brooklyn, Seattle, and Eugene, Oregon, finally settling in Ypsilanti, Michigan, where Patti and I raised our daughters. Social segregation along racial lines prevailed in every location. Patti and I never found the racially integrated Jewish community we sought and tried to create, though we have formed lasting friendships in each place. Our daughters grew up within the pervasive and unsettling atmosphere that our family did not fit within society's dominant lines.

I began my search with questions I knew would defy answers. In what ways was Aunt Rose an outcast, in what ways a rebel? What could explain the different choices made by my father and by Aunt Rose? Without talking directly to them, how would I find out where Aunt Rose and Mr. Arnwine met, why they bought land in southwest Michigan? Did she regret leaving her son, Joey, behind? What were Aunt Rose's reasons for staying in Michigan when, after twenty years, she and Mr. Arnwine divorced? How did she feel about her decisions? Would she have wanted to meet me?

Not long after I found Aunt Rose's death certificate and obituary, I located another piece of evidence of her life in the 1940 federal census, which showed that Zebedee Arnwine and his wife Rose lived in Chicago at 5168 South Michigan Avenue. Everyone on the census page, including Aunt Rose, was coded "Negro." Aunt Rose was coded as working in the home, and Mr. Arnwine as working as a huckster for a vegetable dealer.

With these documents, I felt encouraged that with determination I could find more. While working part-time gigs from my cluttered home office and parenting our teenage daughters, I researched and wrote in the corners of my life. It took years just to find three pictures of Aunt Rose. Unexpectedly—after six years of working on this memoir—I learned that Aunt Rose's younger sister, my Aunt Gertie, kept a private diary during 1933, the crucial year of Aunt Rose's separation from the family.

Writing my aunt's life was an inward-facing process: Though a generation distant, her background is my own. I could hear her sisters' voices, my father's inflections. I listened for echoes within to imagine Aunt Rose.

To write Mr. Arnwine's life, I searched directories, public legal documents, and census records. These shards of his life led me to buried scenes of American history and, specifically, Texas and Oklahoma history. Deep in the archives, I found stories of dispossession, violence, and vulnerability that shaped the contours of my aunt's and Mr. Arnwine's lives. The same themes also shape my own twenty-first-century life.

My Aunt Rose and Mr. Arnwine lived together before, during, and after World War II. This context grabbed me by the throat. They lived with tensions that still echo in my world.

During the war, they bought land on the shore of a small resort lake "reserved for colored people" (according to a county road map published in the 1940s) in Vandalia, Michigan. Paradise Lake had been a covert from brutal racism for over one hundred years, which nurtured what I think of as quiet streams of an iconoclastic, antiracist culture. Their community was not an oasis, but it was racially subversive and necessarily functioned autonomously from most of the country. My Aunt Rose had chosen a life apart from her birth family. On Paradise Lake, she had found a *makom*, a place; a *miklat*, a refuge; and a *mistor*, a hidden place to settle. These biblical Hebrew words resonate throughout this story.

On one of my first visits to Vandalia, I found a street named Arnwine running through a small neighborhood of homes on the south shore of Paradise Lake. Later, I found the deed to the twenty-five acres on which those homes were built, and then a document that had allowed the county government to build a road down the middle of the acreage. The land Aunt Rose and Mr. Arnwine owned with Arnwine Street running down the middle had been platted as the "Arnwine Shores" subdivision. With these facts on the ground, I felt I had found the cornerstone to this story. A place. Aunt Rose had owned a piece of land and had named it.

During the years of my Aunt Rose's long, final illness (in the late 1970s to her death in 1982), I was a union worker in a sewing factory and reeling from the election of Ronald Reagan. Reagan had kicked off his presidential campaign in Philadelphia, Mississippi, where, in the summer of 1964, the civil rights activists Michael Schwerner, Andrew Goodman, and James Chaney had been murdered. Reagan's choice to give his first campaign speech on the subject of "state's rights" was an outright call to white supremacists. The convicted murderers were well-known Klansmen, and when the judge sentenced them to three to ten years in prison for premeditated and cold-blooded murder (though none served more than six years), he said: "They killed one n*****, one Jew, and a white man. I gave them what I thought they deserved." (It seems like the judge might have known that both Schwerner and Goodman were Jewish—but then again, maybe he wouldn't have sentenced their murderers at all if he'd known.)

Aunt Rose and I have negotiated our lives and loves using very different strategies from those of my father and also from each other. My father lived all aspects of his life and raised his children to be safely surrounded by white Jews. He did not need to affirm or deny connection to a home community; he swam within it. Both my parents are descended from Ashkenazi Jews as far back as I can trace.

My Aunt Rose dove into the unknown: In an era of almost complete racial segregation and rising antisemitism, she chose to embrace life in a mostly Christian Black community. Would my life have been different if I'd known she existed? Would her life have been different if she had known she had a niece who needed to know her? When I visit St. Louis and drive along the streets where my family lived, a wave of nostalgia swells, filling me with a feeling of *home*. Even though I've lived far away for more than half my life, I still feel I know this place. Everything about it is of me; there is no separation. There is a spiritual level of connection. For Aunt Rose, this connection was broken.

For her transgressions—marrying Mr. Arnwine, moving away, leaving her son, Joey—Aunt Rose had been excised from her Ashkenazi Jewish family. Yet, when Pesach came, did she refrain from bread? Did she fast on Yom Kippur, the *Vidui* (confessional prayer) echoing in her head? Did she have memories (stories) of the Romania her mother had left only three years before she was born?

Aunt Rose left St. Louis in her late twenties at about the same age I was when I left. Did she, buried in the shadow of the stone church in Vandalia, long for a Hebrew blessing? Did she hear Yiddish in her dreams? Did she miss the kippers, pickled herring, and rye bread my father liked to eat on Sunday mornings? Did she shed the memories? Or did she hold all of it—every scrap and crumb—close to her heart?

Even if I could have interviewed Aunt Rose and Mr. Arnwine, their answers to my questions about their choices to make a life together might have depended on their mood, how much they trusted me, or even the time of day. Their memories of reasons for buying twenty-five acres of land in 1943, far away from any city, would certainly have changed as they aged. Yet, even with the fickleness of memory, I mourn the loss of their stories. For a historian, memories are imprecise and of questionable value; for a storyteller, every memory is a vein of gold.

A family's stories belong to them as a source and form of cultural wealth. The Kinberg stories were lost when emigration from many places in Eastern Europe to St. Louis cut a deep wedge of forgetfulness. And, as I have discovered, so much has been stolen from the Arnwines.

Almost one hundred years ago, the Kinberg and Arnwine stories became intertwined when Aunt Rose and Zebedee Arnwine met. My research for this book contextualizes Aunt

Rose's and Mr. Arnwine's lives within America's multiracial society and its intransigent racism. In the process, I have been able to examine the challenges in my own interracial family life and my search for a home and community, a safe haven within America's racial caste system.

The stories I have found in looking for Aunt Rose's and Mr. Arnwine's lives reveal American history—in East Texas, Oklahoma, Kansas, Missouri, Indiana, Michigan—that has grown increasingly personal to me: I have begun to feel the effects of history in my bones, including events that happened when my Ashkenazi Jewish ancestors still lived in the Pale of Settlement in Eastern Europe. To tell this story of Aunt Rose and Mr. Arnwine, I had to start with the Exodusters of 1877 and the *fusgeyers* of 1904, travelers who have become my ancestors in much the same way as biblical figures—through stories.

Stories—even other people's stories or wholly made-up stories—create memories that are then passed on. I love history, but in the back of my mind, the refrain keeps playing that, in Jewish tradition, cultural memory created by passing down stories is more important than history.

According to the stories Jews tell, when the Israelites returned to Jerusalem after the Babylonian exile (538 BCE), the scribe Ezra cobbled together various manuscripts of the Israelites' origins and redemption from slavery: stories that might have been memories, stories that certainly created memories. These stories were gathered into one scroll, the written Torah, which was copied many times over to be read aloud in gatherings. This is the origin of Jews reading sections of the Torah each week in synagogue, completing a full reading of the five books of Moses each year.

After an emphatic explanation of the work of Ezra and Jewish life thousands of years ago, author Joel Lurie Grishaver writes in *Talmud with Training Wheels* that it doesn't really matter to Jews if Ezra was a real person or if the story of return from the Babylonian exile is historically accurate. Only our memory of these people and events matters, he says.

Even though I have turned these ideas over and over for decades, I struggle to understand the implications of this distinction between history and memory. In *Zakhor: Jewish History and Jewish Memory*, historian Y. H. Yerushalmi explains that memory structures the stories Jews tell about ourselves. Historians gather facts, he writes, and then interpret what they mean. However, with memory, the meaning of the story precedes and determines the events related.

My search for Aunt Rose has led me into lacunae filled with details of Jewish and Black American history, glimpses of other lives I wouldn't have encountered if not for this search. Finding Aunt Rose and the stories of the people she touched in life has given me insight into the social construction of race in America and the consequences of racial designations.

My Aunt Rose died in a hospital in South Bend, Indiana, where she had worked as a nurse's aide. South Bend, though in another state, was a twenty-minute drive from Aunt Rose's home in Vandalia, Michigan. Michiana, the geographic region that includes South Bend in northern Indiana and her home in southwest Michigan, is regarded as having the highest percentage of Black farmers in the rural Midwest. This fact only makes sense in the American context, in which anyone with a single African forebear is designated as Black. But even that *one-drop rule* is contextual: Since at least 1940, the US government had classified my white Ashkenazi Jewish Aunt Rose as Black because she was married to a Black man and lived in Black neighborhoods.

Michiana is also a region with unwritten and irrational yet strictly enforced racial rules. South Bend in the 1940s and 1950s was a growing city with a population of 132,000. It was considerably smaller than St. Louis but still a city with a bustling downtown of small shops and several department stores, many owned by Jewish families—similar to the community culture that Aunt Rose had known in St. Louis.

South Bend, like St. Louis, was also a segregated city in which, for instance, the municipal swimming pool did not allow Black children to swim at the same time as white children. The Black children could only swim once a week or biweekly on a schedule designated by the day before the pool was to be drained, cleaned, and refilled.

I read these details of segregation in South Bend in a personal account by a German Jewish immigrant, Ruth Bachrach Tulchinsky. This account was written for her family and has been digitized as part of the Michiana Jewish Historical Society's records. Ms. Tulchinsky, at age sixteen, had come to South Bend with her religiously observant family. Her book *Life Story* tells of her father making the wise decision to leave Germany with his family in 1937—and the terrible fates of the many relatives left behind.

In addition to *Life Story*, a transcription of Ms. Tulchinsky's interview for the South Bend Civil Rights Heritage

Center is also available online. Her husband, attorney Maurice Tulchinsky, was the only white lawyer the NAACP came to in 1950 to join the team working to desegregate the local public swimming facility, the Natatorium, a struggle that had been going on for almost twenty years. By the time the Tulchinskys became involved in this fight, Mr. Tulchinsky had already signed a petition seeking to overturn Ethel and Julius Rosenberg's death penalty sentences. Ms. Tulchinsky tells of the FBI's visit to the Tulchinskys' home during this period, the interrogation about their reading material, and questions about their associates. In her telling, the FBI and many among the white South Bend community saw working with the NAACP and being a Communist sympathizer as one and the same.

Mr. Tulchinsky lost his law office and many friends in this period, and Ms. Tulchinsky's stories, recorded in her late seventies and eighties, expressed her urgency to convey the connections between her and her husband's values and her own experiences of the Nazis coming to power in Germany. I was struck at the beginning of her oral interview for the Civil Rights Center when Ms. Tulchinsky—at age eighty-seven—said to the interviewer with her slight German accent, "I don't know if you knew that I'm Jewish." I laughed as I heard her say that (could she have possibly thought it wasn't obvious?), yet it made me realize something important. Jews in Michiana assume that anyone outside of the Jewish community must be explicitly told a person is Jewish for that part of their identity to be known. Unlike most of their African American neighbors, Jews assumed they could take advantage of the option to pass as a normative white Christian. For their sense of safety and comfort and for their business and social success, I found Jews in Michiana sometimes adopted a "don't ask, don't tell" policy regarding their Jewishness.

Ruth Anderson Walker—not to be confused with Ruth Bachrach Tulchinsky—is one of the few people I have been able to talk with who knew Aunt Rose. Ms. Walker told me that she suspected that Aunt Rose was Jewish, but she didn't *know*. She thought Arnwine might be a Jewish name, but she never talked to Aunt Rose or Mr. Arnwine about whether they were Jewish.

Through writing these stories, I have learned to have a less rigid conception of Black and Jewish identities and their interplay. I knew from the intimacy of my family and from such theoretical work as Katya Gibel Azoulay's *Black, Jewish, and Interracial: It's Not the Color of Your Skin, but the Race of Your Kin, and Other Myths of Identity* that it was certainly possible that a person could be Black *and* Jewish. I knew when people from the African continent were kidnapped and enslaved, many among them were Christian, Jewish, or Muslim. I also knew that when Jews manumitted people they held in slavery, there was a custom to offer conversion to Judaism to the newly freed. Still, until Ms. Walker said she thought Arnwine might be a Jewish name, I realized I had never considered that Mr. Arnwine could be Jewish. Some years into the writing of this book, I found a Facebook post that claimed that some Arnwine gravestones in Texas are engraved with Stars of David and menorahs. I haven't confirmed this information, yet breaking through the haze of my segregated childhood includes recognizing the possibilities that as Aunt Rose became coded as Black through her marriage to Mr. Arnwine, he in turn became coded as Jewish, and that there may have been Jews among his relatives, or, indeed, Mr. Arnwine could have been Jewish himself.

At a different time, Ms. Walker told me that in 1960, Dr. Martin Luther King Jr. had given a speech in Goshen, a small town just to the southeast of South Bend. Ms. Walker and her husband had gone to hear him. The speech was hosted by Goshen College, a Mennonite institution with a quiet but persistent antiracist history. Goshen itself was a *sundown town*, defined by James W. Loewen, author of *Sundown Towns: A Hidden Dimension of American Racism*, as a town, neighborhood, or community with a wholly white population, created intentionally by systematically keeping out ethnic minorities, through which a Black person could pass during the day but where they best not be discovered after dark. Bringing King there for a day in 1960 (he didn't stay overnight) was a big deal for the college, an event the staff worked on for over a year. Although Goshen, in its pre–Civil War days, was known for being a stop on the Underground Railroad on the way up through southwest Michigan to Canada, the town's racist reputation was well known during Aunt Rose's lifetime. For instance, just a few months after Aunt Rose died in 1982, an interracial Goshen couple living just east of downtown had their car doused with gasoline and torched. If a neighbor walking her dog late at night hadn't seen what was happening and alerted the couple, their house might have been destroyed in addition to their car. Learning of this attack and the open hostility toward interracial couples in the community made me wonder: In the years after Aunt Rose and Mr. Arnwine divorced, did Aunt Rose continue to identify as the (once) white wife of a Black man?

As I conducted research for this book, the racial dynamics in Goshen and South Bend drew my interest. When I looked further into Goshen College, I came across an entry on Goshen in Loewen's database on sundown towns that included this intriguing sentence: "In the 1950s or early 1960s, a Jewish woman in Goshen organized a book club and invited black poets and authors to speak and then had them stay the night, in defiance" of the town's customs.

With some investigation, I found that the "Jewish woman in Goshen" was not Jewish (she was married to a Jewish man); the events referred to happened in 1949 (not the 1950s or 1960s); and the guests were not poets—rather, the guest was the African American sculptor Richmond Barthé, whose Harlem Renaissance work is today represented in the Smithsonian and many other museums. The stories I found related to the "Jewish woman in Goshen," however, sparkled with relevance.

The "Jewish woman" was Lydia Shyne Plaut, whose husband, Sidney Plaut, and father-in-law, David Plaut, owned Plaut's dry goods store on Main Street in Goshen. David emigrated from Germany in 1883 and came to Goshen in 1906 to open a store with the help of his father-in-law, Mortiz Herzog, a fellow German Jewish immigrant. Plaut's dry goods, "Goshen's most talked-about store," was among the "German" storefronts on Main Street, where there were several other Jewish merchants. It seems, however, that David and Sidney kept their Jewish background unspoken of outside of conversations with other Jews, who already knew their identity. The Plauts' Jewish identification was not simple. They were members of a Presbyterian church and did not attend synagogue or follow Jewish religious customs. Yet the Plauts' sense of responsibility to fellow Jews led them to create their most lasting legacy.

In 1935, Sidney married the Irish Catholic actress Lydia Shyne in New York, but it wasn't until 1937 that they took a delayed honeymoon trip to Europe. They were shocked by Mussolini's Italy, and in Germany, Sidney and Lydia were detained and interrogated. Lydia was Jewish in the same way my Aunt Rose was Black—by association in a racist society. When they returned to Goshen, the Plauts began a yearslong project of creating affidavits of sponsorship for more than twenty-eight German Jews, bringing them to Goshen and saving their lives.

The Plauts conducted the rescue in secrecy, and outside of their immediate family, no one knew about their activity. The papers that document their rescue efforts were put into a lockbox and buried beneath a concrete slab in the basement of the Plauts' store. In the 1990s, the store was sold, and during a remodel, the lockbox was unearthed and opened by Sidney's grandson, Steve Gruber, who still lives in the area. Steve worked with filmmakers at Goshen College to create an hour-long documentary titled *Vital Passage: A Holocaust Rescue Story*.

And what of Lydia Plaut's defiance of Goshen's sundown customs? Steve described the event to me:

> My maternal grandmother, Lydia Plaut, was a former New Yorker. In the early '30s in Greenwich Village, as a budding young stage actress, she became very close to African American sculptor Richmond Barthé. She married a man

from Goshen, Indiana, in 1935, but maintained a lively correspondence with Mr. Barthé for over fifty years. In May 1949, he flew to Indiana to stay with the Plaut family. My grandmother invited her (all-female) literary group to meet him and to review the new book that had just been published of his works.

The response was paltry, and she realized it was because of prejudice. One lady confided that her husband didn't want her to attend because it was "highly irregular" for the Plauts to entertain a Negro. My grandmother—ever a genteel crusader—promptly called each of the husbands at their workplaces and told them, "This is a cultural event. And we're proud to have a renowned sculptor visit Goshen. You *and* your wife must come." I guess about two-thirds of the group (with protective spouses) did attend the reception for him at the Plauts' home. My grandfather took pictures of the event.

That visit was iconic. A gay, African American artist who kowtowed to no one stayed with white folks in Goshen for a week—decades before social conventions in the "Maple City" [Goshen] tolerated residents of color.

I have no evidence that the Tulchinskys, the Plauts, and my Aunt Rose knew each other, though I imagine they passed each other on the streets of small-town Michiana. In my mind, they are an intrepid triumvirate, working separately but in some way together to undermine the diseased reign of racism.

As I wrote this story of my Aunt Rose—and myself—I was dedicated to telling the historical facts as I found and verified them. I had no desire to fictionalize—yet I was also aware that my choice of facts and my way of telling the story was determined by what the story means to me. In 2020, the news cycle constantly reminded me that Jews and Palestinians were still fighting in the land of Israel/Palestine, and the COVID-19 pandemic, with its disproportionate effect on the Black community, and then the murder of George Floyd in Minneapolis, made the atmosphere in America increasingly taut, stretched between the fist hold of exposed racism and antisemitism, and at the same time, the counter-efforts to reckon with these terrible systems that shape our human world.

In telling the stories in this book, I am creating memories of Aunt Rose that are useful to me and that, in keeping with Jewish tradition, I hope will be useful to future generations.

I

MY LIFE IN ROSE'S ABSENCE

In the fall of 1960, when I was five, I sat with my parents watching the televised debates between Richard Nixon and John F. Kennedy. I could sense something consequential was happening; I felt but did not understand an unsettling tension emanating from the TV into our family's living room. Some sort of change was in the air. My father was planning a move. Our home in the Jewish enclave of University City outside of St. Louis was a three-story painted white stucco built in 1908, in a neighborhood that was part of the 1904 World's Fair expansion. The fifty-year-old home felt grand to my child self. It had a wraparound porch, with four bedrooms on the second floor and two attic bedrooms in the sloped-ceiling third floor. I had my own bedroom, and my mother's mother lived with us (which meant two of my teenage brothers had to share a room). The neighborhood kids played hide-and-seek in multiple backyards until after dusk, when we could hear our moms calling for us from our front porches.

I understood from overheard adult conversations that we were moving because Black families had moved nearby, too

Dad and me in 1960 at the newly built Jewish Community Center swimming pool near where we would soon move. Personal photo of the author.

close for my father's liking. My father wanted to be ahead of the curve, not taking any chances that I or my remaining school-age brother, Bob, might be in social situations with Black classmates. The 1960 yearbook for University City High School (the school that my three eldest brothers attended) showed no African American students in the senior class out of a total of over five hundred students. Even in 1969, when there were sixty Black graduates out of a class of six hundred, one of the Black students, Judy Gladney, described her experience there as being "a black drop in a sea of white." Her father, a physician, had been the first to integrate the gated University Hills neighborhood in 1965. My family moved out of a nearby neighborhood in the summer of 1963, in the first wave of white flight from University City.

My parents bought into a newly built subdivision in an unincorporated area near Creve Coeur, Missouri. We would drive out to the plot of land on the edge of the city, between newly paved streets and semirural farmland. We watched as the house was built, from poured concrete foundation to freshly sodded lawns.

On January 14, 1963, Rabbi Abraham Joshua Heschel had been in Chicago, speaking at the invitation of Dr. Martin Luther King Jr. at a landmark National Conference on Religion and Race. Even though no one I knew was at the conference and I was too young to even be aware of it, the Civil Rights Movement that the conference helped build was dramatically changing the course of history. Even the private relationship between me, a ten-year-old white Jewish girl, and my fifty-two-year-old father was fundamentally changed by this historic course correction.

Rabbi Heschel, a prolific theologian, philosopher, and activist, was born in Warsaw, Poland, in 1907. He had just finished writing his doctoral dissertation, "The Prophetic Consciousness," in Berlin in 1933 when the Nazis began passing laws restricting all manner of Jewish life. After he immigrated to the United States in 1940, he applied his deeply informed social conscience to America's Civil Rights Movement.

In his opening address at the religion and race conference, Heschel said:

> Racism is worse than idolatry. Racism is satanism, unmitigated evil.
>
> Few of us seem to realize how insidious, how radical, how universal an evil racism is. Few of us realize that racism is man's gravest threat to man, the maximum of hatred for a minimum of reason, the maximum of cruelty for a minimum of thinking.
>
> Let us cease to be apologetic, cautious, timid. Racial tension and strife is both sin and punishment. The Negro's plight, the blighted areas in the large cities, are they not the fruit of our sins? By negligence and silence, we have all become accessory before the God of mercy to the injustice committed against the Negroes by men of our nation. Our derelictions are many. We have failed to demand, to insist, to challenge, to chastise.

Not long after my family settled into our new home thirty miles from the city, I was riding in the front seat of my father's Buick LeSabre, accompanying him to work on a Saturday morning. In this memory, I see myself as about ten years old. My father's used machinery warehouse, Rodell Equipment, located in an industrial part of downtown near the Mississippi River, was a forty-five-minute drive from our home. I loved it when my father occasionally took me to work with him. The huge, grimy machines, some rising to the ten-foot ceilings, scared and thrilled me at the same time. His workplace was a world apart.

On the route, my father drove through a residential Black neighborhood in the city, and I was consumed by sadness and indignation.

Peering out from the Buick's window at the worn redbrick houses, some with boarded windows, I wanted to turn to my father and say, "How can you drive through this neighborhood day after day and just accept that other human beings are living in conditions so much poorer than our own?" But at that moment, my father locked the car doors and opened the glove compartment to allow easy access to a handgun that he, unbeknownst to me at the time, kept there.

That was the moment I lost my father, and my father lost me. Something shattered in my young heart. How could I love and trust someone who witnessed this inequity each day on his drive to work, with no apparent affliction to his soul? His commitment to our safety did not make me feel safe. I needed to know that the evil of racism was as apparent to him as it was to me. My father's approach to our family's safety unmoored me from the whole world I had known. I never found the words to ask him about that moment, to tell him how it affected me.

Although I became disconnected from my father at a young age, I soon found an anchor—via the nightly news—in civil rights and the anti–Vietnam War protests of the midsixties. These reports revealed that I was not alone—that I was but one drop in a sea swell of change. Even though the Black protesters were strangers to me, what they were doing was the only thing that made sense to me—the only way I could imagine living in a world of such inequity.

By the time I was in high school (1969–72), I felt certain I could not live out my life in white, nuclear-family suburbia. Mine was the high school era of jocks, greasers, hippies, and freaks, but I was none of these. In addition, my androgynous disposition became evident during these years. Every morning, after my father left for work, I would go into his closet and pick out one of his many older, white, short-sleeve, button-up work shirts. Over the shirt, I would put on overalls, then my Uncle Nathan's discarded suede sport coat—both very loose fitting. I raided my mother's old clothing too. She had been a tomboy, wearing overalls until she was sixteen, and she still had old dungarees in the bottom of her dresser drawers. My clothing choices were a quiet defiance of gendered expectations. I wanted to be comfortable, not particularly feminine or masculine. A simple, nonbinary uniform appealed as much to me then as it does now, though I've traded in white tailored shirts for black V-neck T-shirts.

In June 1967, when I was twelve, I took my first airplane ride—from St. Louis to New Haven, Connecticut—to attend my brother Myron's graduation from Wesleyan University. While in the airport, I saw the newspaper headlines about Israel's triumph over Arab armies in what would be referred to as the Six-Day War. I shared the relief and pride that blossomed in every Jew I knew. But even then, at twelve years old, my feelings were ruffled with unease:

I believed I was a pacifist, so how could I feel pride over Israel's triumph in war?

During his time at Wesleyan, Myron had been a counselor for conscientious objectors to the Vietnam War draft and had also been accepted into rabbinical school at Hebrew Union College–Jewish Institute of Religion. By August 1967, he had left to spend a year in Israel to help with the aftermath of war, improve his Hebrew, and complete his first of five years of rabbinic training. At twelve, I wasn't able to resolve the contradiction between my pacifism and pride in Israel; rather, I buried the feelings and left the thinking to another time.

On October 15, 1969, the date of the national Moratorium to End the War in Vietnam, I was a fourteen-year-old freshman in high school. I organized with some friends to make black armbands to hand out at school in solidarity with the moratorium. There were only a few of us who wore the armbands, but I knew I was one of millions of Americans who supported the moratorium, one of many voices critiquing US imperialism.

During this period, I read a lot and enjoyed learning, but I was also very restless in my suburban high school. I was nonchalant about skipping school and spending the day reading in a library. Once, while at the library in the old neighborhood, I found a flyer advertising a new alternative high school, Logos, a school "without walls" that used the whole city as its schoolroom, with student-directed learning—the kind of high school I would choose for myself. I was enthusiastic and wanted to apply, but Mom said I needed to ask Dad.

Each evening, my dad would come home from work—often later than my mother expected him—and walk to the liquor cabinet, and then throw back a few shots. After dinner, he'd throw back a couple more and then fall asleep in the lounger in front of the TV.

One evening, I approached him in the lounger to ask about Logos. He snarled. "You're not going there. It's a school for losers, dropouts," he said.

"But not only for dropouts," I retorted, offended by his disdain. "It's for anyone, of any academic ability, who doesn't conform to traditional schools."

But Dad wasn't having it. He exploded with unexpected venom, yelling, "This school is run by a bunch of communists, and you won't go near it—ever."

I knew the argument was over, but I was left perplexed. Communists? Dad was spent; there wasn't anything left to talk about. Something about my wanting to go to Logos touched a raw nerve in my dad, and it came from an emotional, fearful, angry place that made no sense to me but deepened my estrangement from him, from my school, and from my life in the suburbs. Neither Logos nor communism were mentioned again. Yet I craved an uncharted path, and thus I escaped to Paris with Anaïs Nin (through all seven of her diaries) and Henry Miller.

After my first year of college, in 1972–73, during which Richard Nixon was elected president and resigned, I decided I was done with formal school, and I dropped out of the University of Wisconsin. I was frustrated by trying to live, work, and take classes all at the same time. I couldn't do anything well by trying to do it all. I wanted my own apartment, which meant I needed to work more, and I wanted to devise my own course of study, reading books just to learn from them, without having to report to anyone.

So, in the summer of 1973, I moved to Topeka, Kansas, where Myron had taken his first rabbinic pulpit. I got a job driving a mail truck that had been converted into a bookmobile for the Topeka Public Library. I had to stand up and drive the bookmobile from the right side, like I was going to stuff mail into curbside mailboxes. My route was in the rural areas that were too far from the single public library to service the county's patrons, and every day was a quirky adventure. I'd heard that one of the rural households on my route included family members of the Browns, as in the family from the Supreme Court case *Brown v. Board of Education of Topeka*, which in 1954 desegregated public schools in the entire country. When I parked the truck filled with books on the rural road outside of the Browns' house, I could feel the quicksand of history; I was sitting on a surface that included real people who were the same and not the same as the ones who'd changed the world. The facade of the Brown's house was merely a surface disguising the truth inside.

In 1950, seven-year-old Linda Brown was in elementary school in Topeka. She lived in a racially mixed neighborhood but couldn't attend the nearby all-white school and instead had to cross the railroad tracks to catch the bus to the Black elementary school. Meanwhile, the NAACP was organizing Black parents to attempt to enroll students around the country into white-only schools.

The case brought to the Supreme Court included thirteen families from different states. The lead attorney working on behalf of the plaintiffs was future Supreme Court Justice Thurgood Marshall. Of the families' names, Brown came first alphabetically, so the case became known as *Brown v. Board of Education*. By the time the case was settled in 1954, Linda Brown was in middle school, which had been desegregated earlier.

By 1974, when I started working for the Topeka Public Library, with which Linda Brown was also affiliated as a Head Start teacher, she was tired of the publicity and frustrated that so little real progress had been made on racial segregation. Though we were sometimes in the same building, I never spoke to her. Just a few years later, in 1979, she worked with the American Civil Liberties Union (ACLU) to reopen the case, arguing that the district's schools still weren't desegregated.

In 2024, on the seventieth anniversary of *Brown v. Board of Education*, popular historian Heather Cox Richardson wrote about the decision:

> [It] established that the U.S. government would, once and for all, use the Fourteenth Amendment to protect American citizens from discriminatory legislation written by state legislatures. Over the following decades, the Supreme Court used the Fourteenth Amendment to strike down state laws against interracial marriage and gay marriage, and to establish equal rights for women, including the right to abortion. It also ruled the Civil Rights Act of 1964, which prohibited discrimination on the basis of race, color, religion, sex, or national origin, constitutional. That new legal framework, embodied in *Brown v. Board*, both established the equal

rights that were central to the modern era and sparked a backlash against them.

The federal requirement that states desegregate their public schools spurred southern state legislatures to pass laws and resolutions to block or postpone desegregation. Lawmakers also found ways to transfer tax dollars to private schools, which were not covered by the Supreme Court's decision. Attendance at so-called segregation academies exploded. By 1958, more than 250,000 students had migrated to segregation academies, a number that jumped to a million by 1965.

Though the history books will say schools were desegregated one year before I was born in 1955, I only experienced schools and neighborhoods separated by race. In the 1970s, Topeka was just as segregated as it had been in 1954.

While my bookmobile patrons browsed for books, I had time to read. And during that year, I read a lot, mostly about lesbians. In the early 1970s, there was an explosion of books about lesbians. *Lesbian Nation* by Jill Johnston (1973) and *Small Changes* by Marge Piercy (also 1973) were among my favorites. I wasn't out, but I was plotting.

Outside of my nearly perfect job driving the bookmobile, my life in Topeka was a disaster. I knew I was a lesbian, but I had a boyfriend. I was living with a good friend, but she was a heroin user who was sinking away. Myron was a new rabbi who didn't want my messy life to mess with his. He called my parents to come get me, and when they arrived unannounced at my friend's apartment, I didn't resist being shuttled into their car.

I returned to St. Louis, to my parents' home, to my childhood bedroom. At nineteen, this was not a place I wanted to be, and I knew that I needed to hold onto a shred of myself. So, on my first morning back in St. Louis, I borrowed my mother's car and drove to the bookstore on the Washington University campus. I walked up to the first woman I saw, the cashier, and asked about two recently published novels with lesbian protagonists: "Do you have *Rubyfruit Jungle* or perhaps *Patience and Sarah*?" The cashier pointed to the woman at the help desk, who took me to the books (*Yes! There they were!*), and then she asked if I wanted to come over on Wednesday evening for a dinner with her friends' lesbian publishing collective. She mentioned that Barb, the cashier, could use a ride if I had a car. Kalyna, the woman working at the help desk, gave me her phone number and address.

On the next Wednesday, I met a group of out lesbians who wrote poetry; shared cars, meals, clothes, and sometimes lovers; and put out a newsletter for the Lesbian Alliance of St. Louis. Kalyna and Barb, and some of the other women I met that Wednesday, are still my friends, now fifty years later.

I didn't know what a collective was at the time, but I was a quick learner. Collectives made decisions together about how to use resources. Publishing collectives did the work from start to finish: writing, soliciting, designing, typesetting, printing (yes, we had a press), and distributing. All labors of passion for which we made no money. We had other jobs for that.

• • •

Within a year of my return to St. Louis, my father was hospitalized with extreme fatigue. Perhaps my parents knew he was sick when they brought me back from Topeka, but that only seems apparent to me in retrospect. His acute illness, which had been diagnosed as kidney failure, lasted only a few months, and I was too busy with coming out to do more than dutifully visit him when my mother asked. I was visiting him in the hospital in October 1975 when he drew his last breath.

I was twenty at the time of my father's passing, and I hadn't thought of my mysteriously absent Aunt Rose for years. My father's obituary in the *St. Louis Post-Dispatch*, however, included the phrase "Beloved brother of Rose . . ." There she was again—the aunt I had never met. Whoever had written this obituary knew there was a Rose. A Rose we never saw, of whom we never spoke.

It was the year my father died that I first learned my family's version of what happened to my Aunt Rose. That same year, my father's brother Leonard also died. With both brothers' deaths just a few months apart, Leonard's widow, my beloved Aunt Ethel, must have felt more relaxed about keeping family secrets.

With the proximity of our recent losses, the veil between life and death had temporarily lifted, revealing a liminal space where priorities shift. Aunt Ethel took advantage of this moment to ignore a long-held family taboo—she spoke of Aunt Rose. Aunt Rose, she told me, had run off with a Black man, abandoning her young son—my cousin Joey—and the rest of the family. She was rarely seen or heard from again. Joey was raised by another of my father's sisters, my Aunt Gertie. I knew my cousin Joey well, along with his two sons, who were just a couple of years younger than me. They had always been among the swarm of cousins I regularly saw.

Hearing about Aunt Rose this time, the reality stuck: My father had a secret sister Rose. There was another aunt, and her life had led her away from the family. Until that moment, the St. Louis Kinbergs had felt cocooned in a sticky milkweed pod from which I alone had burst. But in an instant, I saw that another Kinberg had left the pod years before. It was thrilling to know that I was not alone, that another Kinberg woman had lived an unconventional life, had challenged the status quo, had followed her heart, had defied racial segregation. Learning about Aunt Rose was an infusion of oxygen.

I could take a deep breath knowing my own unruly inclinations were not a complete anomaly in my family. At twenty years old, I liked to walk deep into the woods until I was deliberately lost and then use my wits to find my way to a familiar road or landmark. I felt comforted that someone so familiar with my family, an aunt, had also felt the stirring sensation of leaping into the unknown. Yet Aunt Rose was also a stranger to me. That she had not returned, or was not allowed to return, filled me with a sadness I wanted to assuage by finding her.

I understood that "abandoning the family" was only one way to interpret Aunt Rose's story. Aunt Rose moved away during the Great Depression and thereafter lived her life among Black people; at the same time, my father and the rest of the family had exiled her from our family. In the early twentieth century, as Ashkenazi Jews like my family members emerged from the trauma of immigration, each made decisions on how to act and position themselves within

America's racial hierarchy. Aunt Rose and my father had made very different choices.

At the time when my father died, I was consumed with the feeling that his anti-Black racism had turned him into a relic of a human being. I was disappointed and angry at him but also aware that if I wanted my own life to be different from his, I needed to commit myself to what we then called "unlearning" the racism that permeated my personal life and every aspect of life in America.

I was also coming into my identity as a young lesbian and feminist at that time. A poster quoting Mao Tse-tung that stated "women hold up half the sky" hung in the bedrooms of my friends, and I had heard lines from Muriel Rukeyser's poem "Käthe Kollwitz" that challenged, "What would happen if one woman told the truth about / her life? / The world would split open." At twenty, these beliefs shaped my world.

I urgently wanted to hear Aunt Rose's side of this story, and I resolved to find her. It took a very long time. With Aunt Rose's vague shadow always at my periphery, I continued to read a lot, and I began to write and edit.

In 1977, my lesbian collective published an issue of our journal, *Moonstorm*, on the theme of "food," covering topics ranging from food stamps, waitressing, and farm labor to harmful additives and corporate control of the food chain. I wrote an article about managing a neighborhood food co-op, and another woman wrote about "living on the land" in a lesbian land collective. She wrote:

> None of the 5 of us now living here put in any of the initial money for the land; there was a down payment made by

> one woman who moved away 6 months later, and the mortgage payments are made by whoever is here and by whatever means possible: a hay operation for a neighbor (cutting, raking and baling the hay) paid one payment; the sale of cattle and milk paid for another few. There have always seemed to be people who donate part of the payment, and for one or more of the people here to move to a city to make the money.
>
> We live frugally so the money usually goes a long way, plus our food trip here is a lot different than in the city. We eat out of the garden, growing fresh vegetables to eat, freeze, and can, from the wild fruits we have around, and we have a milk cow, which gives us milk, cream, butter, yogurt, cottage cheese, ice cream, and sometimes hard aged cheese. We also have chickens to give us eggs (which can be very inconsistent) and goats for milk and/or meat (for those who eat meat).

The idea of learning to grow my own food took hold of me, and by the fall of that year, I'd moved to Dragonwagon in the Ozarks, to live on a lovely 140-acre, communally owned plot of land with a constantly changing, endlessly fascinating collective of lesbians. On the farm, I explored my ecological values, my nature-based spirituality, my desires for simplicity and self-sufficiency.

I planted a field of comfrey and tried to support myself by selling mail-order reusable menstrual sponges. I bought a large number of small natural sponges from a pottery supply warehouse, wrote a booklet on why and how to use them, and put ads in lesbian publications around the country. The sponges worked quite well in collecting the flow, but rinsing the sponges in public bathroom sinks was an unforeseen

Covers of various issues of Moonstorm, *which was published from 1973 to 1980.*

downside (the stares!) and the eco-friendly, reusable menstrual sponge did not catch on. When my financial plan didn't work out, I went to work at a shoe factory about thirty miles away from the farm.

It didn't take very long to learn how polluted the air of rural Missouri could be. Early one morning as I was catching a ride to the shoe factory with some locals, the conversation turned to their enjoyment of nighttime "coon" hunting (that is, looking for Black people to terrorize). I sensed they were baiting me to join in the merriment. I knew I could never let myself be alone with that crew again. When spring came, I packed my clothes and typewriter and headed back to St. Louis. Thus ended my first of three moves to rural areas, where I lived amid farmland, with enough space to grow large gardens.

I loved the challenges of country living, but they were far from fulfilling. I also thrived on interacting with people of different races and ethnic backgrounds in the city, and I missed it. The culture of white rural America was not for me, even if I loved waking to the sounds of chickens and goats rather than traffic. My childhood in the all-white suburbs of St. Louis was more than enough segregation for my lifetime.

With six months of sewing heel tabs at the shoe factory behind me, I could put "sewing machine operator" at the top of my resume, and St. Louis still had several garment factories. Although I was never very good at piecework, I didn't hate it either.

After settling back into my home-in-the-city lesbian collective in St. Louis, I applied for work at Modern Jacket, located in the Merchandise Mart (now upscale condos) on Tenth and Washington. When I entered the outer office for my job interview, I sat in a chair next to two African American women, a factory worker with a bleeding eye and an older woman dressed in a skirt and jacket business suit. They were called in to speak to the manager before me. He left the door open so everyone in the office could hear the older woman, who I learned was the union representative, Ora Lee Malone (whom I later came to love and know well). I heard her explain how a broken needle had cut the other woman's eye. When they were finished, the manager called me in.

Mr. Manager took one look at me and my name and asked if I was related to the other Kinbergs he knew. Evidently his son or nephew played baseball with one of my brothers, and he knew my father and other details about my family. After establishing our common Jewish community credentials, he asked why I wasn't looking for an office job. I assured him that I wanted to sew, and then expressed some concern about safety on the shop floor to make it clear that I had overheard pieces of his conversation with the two women who'd been in his office before me.

I asked him what had happened to her bleeding eye, and he replied, "I didn't really look at it. There was too much brown all around it." His racism hit me like a poison dart, and I was sickened by his assumption that he could openly express it to me because we were members of the same tribe, or even perhaps because he knew my father. I signed the papers to start work the following Monday, but my four years at Modern Jacket were shadowed by this encounter.

The owner of Modern Jacket was Siegmund (Siggy) Halpern, who was born in Vienna, Austria, in 1919, and escaped after the Anschluss, when Austria was annexed by

Nazi Germany. During the year when I started at Modern Jacket (1978 or 1979), Siggy was president of the St. Louis Jewish Federation.

There were only two other Jews on the shop floor: Marta and Oscar. Marta was a recent immigrant from the Soviet Union. She had been an engineer in the USSR, but now she pushed a cart between the sample room and the sewing floor, a job for which the bosses paid her two dollars an hour. Her pay was then subsidized up to minimum wage by a Jewish resettlement agency. The other Jew was Uszer (Oscar) Ozarowski, a tailor who sewed samples and whose thin, bent frame stood out when he would occasionally shuffle around the shop floor. I learned from his obituary in 2010 that he had been born in Poland and that he had "spent five years in the Lodz ghetto before being sent to the concentration camps. He saw the notorious Dr. Josef Mengele, and watched his mother and sister herded into gas chambers as they yelled: 'Revenge' and 'Don't forget us.'"

I was assigned to be a top stitcher, hemming cheap winter coats. At exactly 7 a.m., a bell rang and the machines were turned on, initiating a scream and clamor that continued for the next eight hours, minus breaks and lunch, when the machines were all simultaneously turned off without need of the obligatory bell. My coworkers included immigrants from Greece, Korea, and Italy but many were Black women from St. Louis. Dorothy Jackson sat at the front of my line, setting a pace that only her determined stamina could keep up. Dorothy sewed twice as many coats as anyone else. Everyone counted. The whole section drew from the same stack of bundles, so when orders were down and there wasn't enough to fill a whole day's work, Dorothy's speed piqued chords of resentment.

Little Aretha (Dorothy called her Grandma) had a station off to the side, turning the coats right side out for hemming. Aretha would start the chatter that kept us all moving through the paces of the day. Hot water pipes running along the walls were used to keep coffee warm. Winter coats were only sewn in summer, with St. Louis heat keeping the factory over ninety degrees most days. The old-timers swore hot coffee kept you cool.

High up on the wall above Dorothy's head, in between huge windows too dirty to see out, was the clock. The choking dust in the air, filling the corners and ledges, had probably been there for fifty years, since the factory had opened.

Modern Jacket was a union shop. Everybody paid their dues; most even made their tired way to the union meeting up at the hall once a month. The union hall was just a block from the shop, and you could catch the bus home from there just as easily as in front of the factory. I went diligently to the meetings, barely repressing my earnest, almost romantic excitement at being a union member. At the meetings, the women spoke their minds; they were invariably angry at the union, feeling cheated and betrayed, but they hated the bosses more—no question about it.

Next to the shop's time clock, where everyone lined up to punch in and out, above the water fountain, and across from the elevators and glass-enclosed office, was the union bulletin board. When I started working at Modern Jacket, the only notice ever posted there was for the monthly union meeting, tacked right in the center.

The bulletin board was a perfect spot, I thought, for the posters produced by my lesbian print collective. The first poster I anonymously displayed was a drawing based on an archival photo of women striking in the 1920s, the year the union was formed. "They fought for it. We can't afford to lose it. Defeat the 'Right to Work,' Rip-off," the poster said.

A few months later, after the right-to-work legislation was defeated, I posted another of the collective's creations: my friend Barb Goedde's drawing of the crescent-shaped public hospital on the Northside, one of the nation's oldest training hospitals for Black nurses and doctors. The poster read, "Join the barricade. Save Homer G. Phillips Hospital. Stop closures of public hospitals."

In the 1970s, the residential streets of St. Louis's Northside were an unknown world to most white people. Remote from even the imagination of St. Louis's white citizens, Homer G. Phillips sat in the middle of the Northside, an icon of the Black community whose massive presence attested to both white racism and Black resilience, as the 2018 movie *The Color of Medicine: The Story of Homer G. Phillips Hospital* describes.

Along one side of the hospital was a street of cold-water flats, while the adjoining streets had fine old three-story brick residences, with lead-glass doors and carved-wood entrances. All the corner liquor stores had plywood windows, iron bars, and steel gates. Catty-corner to the hospital was a fourteen-story nursing home filled with elderly Black men and women, all with stories to tell. They came out to the twenty-four-hour vigil to keep the city from closing the hospital, which gave all of us younger folks a lot of time to listen.

A Tiamat Press poster on voting against a right-to-work initiative in 1978. It was defeated, with over 60 percent of voters voting "no." Artwork by Barb Goedde.

The poster of the Homer G. Phillips Hospital hung on the Modern Jacket union bulletin board for over a year. I was proud of it, but my political fervor and lesbian identity kept me tongue-tied. Though my tailored slacks, button-down white shirts, and cropped hair said a lot, I was in the closet with my coworkers about my after-work political activities, and everything else about my life.

Still, the hum and clatter of my machine connected me to the 114 women on the floor, working on pockets, sleeves, linings, collars, backs, fronts, hems, and topstitching. Sitting at the machine day after day, I felt a physical connection to the Jewish factory workers, unionists, socialists, visionaries, and revolutionaries whose stories I had read in dozens of books.

Only a few of my coworkers were old enough to remember other Jewish operators, both women and men. Mary Lavac, who sat two machines behind me, remembered her birthplace in Lebanon as well as many Jewish friends from years back. By 1978, most of the machine operators were white and Asian immigrants.

All these years later, I remember Oscar, Siggy, and Marta, whose lives embodied the Jewish traumas of my home community, along with Mary, Dorothy, Aretha, and my other coworkers, and I feel a cluster of tension in my chest. I am a member of multiple communities, all with separate concerns, with members whose social lives are so different from each other they almost speak different languages. Although I was completely at home in an interracial, lesbian activist collective during this part of my life, at work I was always an oddball, not as comfortable with code-switching as I wish I could have been.

My union, the Amalgamated Clothing and Textile Workers Union, had been founded by immigrant Jews. The Jewish unionists had carved a space into history for me. At that

The poster about Homer G. Phillips Hospital still hangs in my office.

time, reading history books felt like seeing a pentimento: I'd squint, and the histories I read about turn-of-the-century Jewish socialists were suddenly describing the lesbian collectives I was so familiar with.

When I found the works of secular Jewish historian Simon Dubnow, my life began to make some sense to me. "The historian's task consists of establishing the organic connection between the separate links of the historical process," he wrote. I was not a historian—but I was a link.

At home, in the lesbian collective house we'd named Thornapple, our busy and complicated comings and goings did not help us blend into the neighborhood; instead, our tales of being harassed are infamous and recorded in

Mary Maxfield's chapter, "'Together We Can Make a Safe Home': Space, Violence, and Lesbian Organizing in 1970s St. Louis," in the book *Left in the Midwest: St. Louis Progressive Activism in the 1960s and 1970s.* One memory: A blond, ten-year-old boy who lived next door had become obsessed with the "lezzies" on his block. One Saturday afternoon, I woke up from a nap to hear him cry from his rooftop, "Clare is a les-bi-an, Clare is a les-bi-an." He kept it up for several hours, until the sun went down. I lived in the house for ten years, and the harassment never abated.

During my time in the house, in the summer of 1980, I caught a Greyhound bus from St. Louis to San Francisco, the gay center of the universe. On the day of my arrival, I saw a poster at Modern Times Bookstore for a "people's fair." The day of the fair was sunny, the jugglers were out, and the voices of a Black women's a cappella group punctuated the air. I was awed and enticed, and a little overwhelmed.

Every left-wing political group was at the fair with their wares, all with the message that if only US imperialism were halted, the marginalized peoples of the world would be free to fill every space with fresh, colorful designs and new, exciting rhythms. Posters, pamphlets, bumper stickers, and incense were for sale, one booth after another. I was feeling lightheaded, the free atmosphere so different from the closed Midwest where I'd lived for all of my twenty-five years.

A red-and-black poster caught my eye. It took me a moment to focus on it. The black was an outline of Israel; the red, a blood-covered dagger stuck through the middle of the state. I took a sudden step back, transfixed by the poster, unable to comprehend its message. Silently, something in me said, "No." And I moved on to the next booth, but with my spirits greatly dampened. Until that moment, my attachment to Israel had existed outside of my critique of American imperialism.

The next day, I returned to Modern Times Bookstore and found an old copy of a magazine in which several Jewish leftists debated the right of Israel to exist, arguing in the style so common among the male left at the time: confident and harsh, going for the throat. I at once admired the writers for the conviction of their prose, and I was intimidated by their knowledge but unconvinced by their arguments. I wanted to meet the writers, hear their analysis and arguments in person. Unfortunately, the magazine was two years old and had folded.

The poster and the magazine that had folded made me want to get back to St. Louis, where I was on more familiar ground. The San Francisco Bay Area was an eye-opening place to visit, but in St. Louis, among my radical and multiracial lesbian friends, I felt I could untangle my feelings about my experience at the people's fair.

In the fall of 1980, on the strength of his call to racists, Ronald Reagan was elected to the presidency. Immediately, my union began working on a large "jobs and justice" march on the nation's capital organized primarily by the NAACP, the American Federation of Labor and Congress of Industrial Organizations, and the United Auto Workers. In September 1981, I joined a busload of my fellow union members to travel to Washington, DC.

The union-chartered tour bus was full yet comfortable. So that we could be ready to march early in the morning, the ride to DC was overnight. Near the center of the bus, several rows of seats swiveled to face each other with pull-up tables in between, a good setup for a game of cards, which we played through the long nighttime hours.

Sometime around 3 a.m., a guy across the table asked me, "What are you?"

I assumed I knew what he meant—that he was asking whether I was Jewish. My olive complexion and dark curls had often elicited this question, and I didn't know then that there were many possibilities behind his question, and many possible answers. My assumption that I was being asked about being Jewish reveals both my self-consciousness and my lack of exposure to the wider world.

Racial ambiguity in America makes people uncomfortable. Our laws have always required us to identify our race. And socially, we want to know what people "are" and how they self-identify. Even though race is a social construction, the community in which a person is rooted, the cultural language one is familiar with, and one's expectations of other people's assumptions are just the tip of what matters about our racial identity in social situations. When the man across the table asked, "What are you?" I felt exposed, and I had to answer. I froze for a moment, awash in a vague dread that if I revealed my Jewishness, the camaraderie I'd felt during the card game would be spoiled. I pulled out my go-to in such situations and grabbed for the ethnic diversion, "Well, I'm part Romanian and part Russian." My truthful yet evasive answer brought a skeptical snort and a round of side-eyes.

"Okay, yeah, I'm Jewish," I said, and everyone laughed and went on with the game. No one else seemed bothered, but the exchange made me uncomfortable, and I soon excused

My coworkers in the sewing factory and I on our way to the Solidarity Day march on Washington, which focused on jobs and freedom, in 1981. I am second from left, standing in the back.

myself and found an empty seat near the dark front of the bus where almost everyone else was asleep. In a few minutes, I was joined by Henry, a young lanky coworker I knew from the shipping department.

"Why were you so reluctant to tell them you're Jewish?" he asked quietly, almost as if my own conscience were speaking to me.

"I don't know," I answered. But Henry wasn't having it.

"Look," he said, "if you could be proud of being who you are, proud of being Jewish, it would make it easier for me to be proud of being Black. Don't be afraid to be who you are. I need that from you." He didn't wait for an answer; when he was done speaking, he got up and left me to stew.

It was a watershed moment. I realized I had a pent-up fear of letting non-Jews know I am Jewish, and Henry had given me a good reason to face this fear and stare it down. I had used my real but barely known Romanian heritage to elide my Jewish identity. I never did that again.

With the push from Henry to more publicly own my Jewishness and my obsessive reading about Jewish radicals while being active in my union, my identity and activist priorities began to shift. In 1982, war in the Middle East forced a lasting change.

In late summer of 1982, I sat at my kitchen table reading three newspapers: the *St. Louis Globe-Democrat*, the *St. Louis Post-Dispatch*, and *The New York Times*. Each had, in its own way, become essential daily reading since June 6, the day Israel had invaded Lebanon. Yet beyond murmuring, "It's awful," "How could this be happening," I didn't really have anyone to talk to about Israel. I had many Jewish friends, but we didn't talk about Israel or Jewishness. I picked through the papers, silently. As the daily ritual extended into weeks, a persistent awareness of everything related to Israel enveloped my consciousness.

On August 24, after Israel's siege of Beirut but before the massacres in the Palestinian refugee camps Sabra and Shatila, Rabbi Jerome Grollman of the United Hebrew Temple, "the oldest Reform congregation west of the Mississippi," wrote a letter to the editor of the *St. Louis Post-Dispatch* with the headline "Beirut Was a Disaster That Must Not Be Repeated." He began the letter with, "Israel's invasion of Lebanon was a Jewish disaster," also calling it, "a Jewish disgrace."

Even then, in August 1982, Rabbi Grollman knew how the Jewish community was going to divide over this. "Courageous and dedicated Jews are beginning to speak out.

Admittedly we are in the minority, but we are a growing number. True, we are somewhat helpless. World Jewish opinion is controlled by the Begin-Sharon establishment through such instruments as the Conference of Presidents of Major Jewish Organizations."

Rabbi Grollman ended his letter to the *Post-Dispatch*, "Once before, we who are Jewish invoked the slogan: 'Never again.' We must now invoke it a second time. In the name of God, in the name of humanity, in the name of Torah, in the name of every Jewish value we hold sacred . . . never again must Israel be a party to such carnage. Never again must the Jewish people justify such violence."

The backlash of the St. Louis Jewish community's legacy leaders against Rabbi Grollman was led by Bob Cohn, longtime editor of the *St. Louis Jewish Light* newspaper, who in an editorial on September 8, 1982, still a week before Sabra and Shatila, wrote that Rabbi Grollman "selected as his forum to assail Israel the editorial page of the *St. Louis Post-Dispatch* which for years has been among the most anti-Israel and pro-Arab forums in America. In issue after issue, [*Post-Dispatch*] editorials consistently denounce Israel for every alleged infraction while remaining curiously silent on Arab atrocities." Cohn ended his editorial, "We have a profound moral obligation to avoid joining or offering to put a rabbinic stamp of approval on the growing anti-Israel lynch mob."

Cohn's stinging statement of ridicule and condemnation used some powerful tools. Trumpeting support for Israel as a "moral obligation" was meant to shut down any discussion. Cohn then heightened the emotional stakes with an alarming subversion of the phrase "lynch mob," using it as a metaphor for the few who broke from offering uncritical support for Israel's military offensive.

In truth, Rabbi Grollman was not "anti-Israel," and no one was being hanged for supporting Israel. Yet the extrajudicial murder (the literal meaning of the uniquely American term *lynch*) of Black people was then and remains now a reality. In 1982, a federal antilynching bill first introduced to Congress in 1900 was still forty years from becoming law (President Joe Biden signed the Emmett Till Antilynching Act on March 29, 2022). By inventing an "anti-Israel lynch mob," Cohn undermined the power of language to describe anti-Black violence. Cohn's rhetoric worked to deepen an already growing political wedge between St. Louis's Black and Jewish communities, sabotaging Black and Jewish collaboration.

In mid-September 1982, on the day that the news of the massacres in the Palestinian refugee camps Sabra and Shatila was spread across the kitchen table, I forced myself to read out loud *New York Times* columnist Thomas Friedman's very long and detailed eyewitness account. "The grisly task of clearing out the bodies from a camp still reeking with death took place as new information emerged about the extent of the massacre of Palestinian civilians and the role played by Israeli forces in the events of the last four days," I read quietly, the images burning my throat.

My housemates, on their way to breakfast and work, stopped to listen. When I read that it appeared the Israeli army had aided the massacre by permitting the Falangists into the camps knowing full well their intentions, one of the women said, "Well, what did you expect?" and the other bustling women echoed, "Yeah, really."

I shrank into my seat, flushed with confusion, then bolted for the back door.

I loved our little swatch of a yard, even though the grass was patchy and full of weeds, with trees growing on either side creating too much shade for anything to thrive. The wind blowing through the leaves was soothing as I searched for an effective and appropriate response to my housemate's stinging, offhand comment. "What did you expect? What did you expect?" repeatedly thudded in my head. I did not have an articulate answer—only that I did expect something else. Or, rather, I hadn't expected this. I felt unprotected and empty, without resources. Accused and defenseless. This was the first time I realized that, though I had many Jewish friends, none of my housemates were Jewish.

I needed other Jews to talk to, and in my search to find Jews with whom I could try to untangle my thoughts, I found a deep chasm between my Jewish friends, who were unconnected to any Jewish organizations, and other Jews—the ones who read the *St. Louis Jewish Light*.

My friends were consumed by a moral crisis revealed by Israel's actions, by the many thousands of Lebanese and Palestinians who were killed during the invasion and siege, the indefensibly disproportionate loss of non-Jewish life. Despite my attachment to Israel, I (and my friends) had been shaped by the Vietnam War and the Civil Rights Movement. On the other side, the *Jewish Light* and all the legacy Jewish organizations were consumed with defending Israel. There was no bridge. Jewish congregations, organizations, and agencies betrayed and kicked to the curb those of us whom Rabbi Grollman had identified as the dedicated

Jews who were just beginning to find our voices, and each other.

I continued to read the *Jewish Light*, which maintained that every Jew agreed, or should agree, that public criticism of Israel was outside of the moral boundaries of Jewish responsibility. At the same time, I reached out to my many Jewish friends who had, like me, avoided Israel discussions for too long and thought a full public airing of these issues was needed. Although there was an obvious chasm in the community, I refused to become an outcast from the Jewish community in which I'd grown up. Through the lesbian community, I had friendships and connections to Jews who shared my antiwar and human rights values. But the threat of being an outcast sat on my shoulder. Aunt Rose had crossed a red line of her era, an interracial marriage. I was yet to find out whether agitating for Palestinian lives was the red line of my era.

At the time, United Hebrew Temple (UH), led by Rabbi Grollman, was the only Jewish congregation within the St. Louis city limits; the other congregations had already followed the majority of Jews, who had participated in white flight and moved farther west into the suburbs. My oldest childhood friend had his bar mitzvah at UH. Its columned, classical facade and huge domed sanctuary with three thousand velveteen seats were familiar—yet it was not a space in which I found comfort. I never spoke to Rabbi Grollman about his letter to the *Post-Dispatch*, but out of a feeling of solidarity, I applied to teach in the temple's religious school and was hired to teach seventh-grade Sunday school.

Working closely and teaching with other Jews who were active in the Jewish community conjured in me an ambivalent attraction. Part of me felt quite at home teaching Jewish kids, but on the other hand, could a lesbian and feminist free spirit fit into a slightly musty classroom of young people who didn't want to be there? It was almost like being lost in a musky woods; the challenge drew me in.

Friends often ask me why my Jewish identity is so important to me. I don't know what to say other than: "This is my place." My identity has given me a perch, created an observatory where I can view, or try to view, all of Jewish history along with the adjacent people and places. The location of my perch—my viewing point—is every place Jews have lived. The time frame is thousands of years.

I love the work I do as a Jewish educator and editor, passing on a thousands-year-old spiritual/cultural heritage, adding my two cents at the same time. For most of this time, God hasn't played a conscious role in my Jewish writing or teaching beyond trying to understand the way Jews have conceptualized God differently over the centuries. My approach to God has been secular and academic.

In the early 1980s, I was enchanted with the writings of Mordecai Kaplan, the founder of Reconstructionist Judaism, who eschewed a transcendent or supernatural deity in favor of understanding God as a unifying quality or force through which humans can be part of a process of integration, harmony, and self-fulfillment. Kaplan's teaching that Judaism is an evolving religious civilization opens the door to recognizing and encouraging evolving understandings of God. My own faith in a unity and interconnectedness of all of creation, and my belief that I am a particular emanation of God, brings me joy and provides purpose, helping me live a worthy life.

When I led children's services for the Jewish High Holidays, I put up a chuppah and asked the kids to imagine that the Jewish wedding canopy had become the open-sided tent of our ancestors Sarah and Abraham. This symbol of the open tent is powerful in Judaism, standing in for many deeply embedded ideas. The open tent is a metaphor for Judaism's face to the world. We don't leave the tent to proselytize. Jews and non-Jews passing by the tent may *ta sh'ma*: come and listen / come and learn. Taking permanent shelter under the tent is a commitment that is available, and there are refreshments in the tent—hospitality is a mitzvah. But we don't chase after the passersby.

I don't really know if Christianity is fundamentally different in this regard, but it seems that way to me. Christians have proselytized to me, like most Jews I know, and I have resented having to put up a resistance, even (especially) when the proselytizer has good intentions. As a preteen, I remember attending a fun song fest that ended with the leaders handing out "one way" poster-board hands with a finger pointing to the sky. The meaning of the one-way symbol, that salvation is only available through accepting Jesus as the son of God, slowly dawned on us Jewish kids. I felt tricked, frightened, and then angry. And I already knew there is more than one way to salvation because it is obvious to Jews who live among Christians, Muslims, and others that there are many paths to God, to a righteous life, to purpose, joy, and redemption.

I'm comfortable with my faith, and I think of myself as open to others whose faith is different from mine. Many

Jews I know incorporate Buddhist and other meditation practices not originated in Judaism into their Jewish practice. And I know that, historically, Jewish practice has been permeable. Many years ago, my beloved sister-in-law Alice Haya Kinberg *z'l*, who grew up in Morocco before escaping to Israel in the 1960s, expanded my mind with stories about Jewish Sufis in Morocco. Most Sufis in Morocco were Muslim, but their practice of ecstatic spinning connecting them to God was also practiced by some Jews, another example of cultural practices with spiritual meaning being shared by people of different religions.

As a child, I occasionally went with my mother to the Reform Temple for prayer services, yet I didn't like repeating words I didn't understand or believe. My deepest feeling during Hebrew prayer was confusion. As I watched my mother listen to the chanted prayers, I wondered what she was feeling. Did she believe in God?

I never asked my mother about God, afraid that if she did believe, I still wouldn't understand. And if she didn't believe in God, I worried that I would be overcome with the emptiness of the prayers.

Now, I savor opportunities to ask questions.

I imagine that other Jews do feel spiritually connected, or at least nostalgic, when they hear the Rosh Hashanah melodies. When they hear Kol Nidre on the eve of Yom Kippur, I imagine Jews—other Jews—feel something vital and necessary.

Despite my trouble with Jewish prayer, I don't remember ever wanting to shed my Jewish identity, and I still occasionally attend prayer services. I've found meaning and purpose in bringing whatever I have to offer to the four-thousand-year-old project of Jewish civilization. Connecting to other Jews and experiencing the world as a Jew tethers me.

I met my wife Patti around 1980. She was my first serious relationship with a non-Jew, but she quickly made up for that by devouring one of my favorite books, Nora Levin's *While Messiah Tarried: Jewish Socialist Movements, 1871–1917*. I didn't know anyone else, Jewish or otherwise, who had read this book. I still smile when I think of how we discussed it.

When we first met, we both knew we wanted to raise children eventually. As a lesbian couple, the decision to adopt was fraught in many ways. Adoption into a two-female-parent household was illegal in some places and was a liminal situation everywhere else. But we knew lesbian couples who'd successfully adopted, so we had role models and mentors to guide the way.

Adoption is a very intentional way to form a family. You fill out forms to indicate the type of children you are willing to take responsibility for: their age, race, and potential level of medical issues. Patti and I talked long and hard about adopting Black children into our multiracial, Jewish, lesbian family. We knew it would be hard on the children, and twenty-five years later, we are still learning how hard it has been for them. But looking back, we all feel it was meant to be, and the girls have survived to become adults in a society that has changed relatively little in terms of social segregation.

Patti and I knew that the National Association of Black Social Workers was vehemently opposed to Black children being placed in white families for any reason. We understood and supported their position, which was published in 1972 and extends to today.

Our decision to adopt Black infant girls was predicated on our already being an interracial family, though not without reservations. Patti had been raised in a family that she believed was white until her teenage years, when she and her siblings discovered that their mother and grandmother were Creole and had come to St. Louis from Louisiana to pass for white. Patti's mother was a child when they came north, and it wasn't until the 1970s that she reconnected with her Black and Creole relatives. Even though Patti had been raised to believe she was white, knowing the truth about her mother's family explained so many things: the unique smells of Creole cooking in family kitchens, her grandmother's "French" accent, the family's changed names, their lack of known relatives, and more. In forming our family with the intentionality of adoption, Patti had no desire to revert to the fictions required when her grandmother passed for white. Being a more visibly interracial family felt like reconnecting to the truth for us and seemed right for our family.

We committed to raising our daughters with extended family and community that was Black and Jewish, and we sought support from our families and lesbian friends to fulfill these commitments. All of this was easier to imagine than to live.

We made a lot of mistakes. Gymnastics, karate, T-ball, soccer, dance classes—for each, we settled for only signing up the kids if they weren't the *only* kids of color in the group. But we could have done so much more. We didn't access the churches and community centers where the majority of kids were Black, for example. There were many times we didn't challenge our own comfort zones, which tended toward multiracial environments. In places where racial segregation is the norm, exposing your Black children to only those few multiracial situations is not enough. With the kids, we made a habit of counting the number of Black people every time we entered a space, believing the number was proportional to the relative comfort our girls were likely to experience.

When Patti and I got the call in 1998 that a girl had been born who needed an adoptive family—a girl who would become our daughter—we were living on an idyllic few acres outside of Eugene, Oregon. We had abundant plum and apple trees and a half-acre garden that we'd fenced against the deer and our large, capricious dogs. We heated the small home with a wood stove and watered the growing vegetables with an elaborate system fed from the well, from which we also drank, in a corner of the garden. In our five years there, we'd painted the house inside and out, built a pottery studio for Patti, put in all new electrical wiring, and fed ourselves almost entirely from our own garden. Yet if we were to become the parents of a Black child, we knew we would need to move. We needed to live somewhere a Black child could be in Black community—ideally a rural area or a small town. The place we dreamed of seemed to not exist. I didn't know then how racially mixed, rural towns were deliberately hidden from scrutiny.

We adopted our younger daughter in early 2001 and resolved to move from Oregon before the girls started school. Oregon, where our family was regarded as an attention-grabbing oddity and where the girls were often not seen beyond the color of their skin, was not the place to raise them. When our oldest was still an infant in our arms, I took her on an errand to the local supermarket. As we were walking across the parking lot returning to the car, a young white guy yelled from two rows away to catch my attention, "Did you just get that from Africa?" In pure Oregonian style of trying to cover racism with hipness, he added something like, "That's really beautiful, man." I was still vulnerable enough as a brand-new parent to start to answer him, and my mouth opened and closed before the knifepoint of his racism reached bone.

Patti and I began our search for a new home by compiling lists of the "best cities for interracial families," and we added these into our other criteria: affordable and friendly to lesbian families. The affordable part nixed all of California and many large cities. We'd never lived in the South and, given its classic racist history and our ignorance of Southern life, we were reluctant to search there. We wanted to get a feel for the places we considered, so we took road trips to Evanston, Illinois; Yellow Springs, Ohio; Montclair, New Jersey; Mount Airy, Pennsylvania; and Ann Arbor, Michigan. Patti got a scholarship to attend graduate school at the University of Michigan, which finally made the decision for us.

Unbeknownst to me at the time, my Aunt Rose had moved to Michigan sixty years earlier. She and her husband settled on the shores of Paradise Lake in 1943, when she was thirty-five years old and he was already forty. Mr. Arnwine and Aunt Rose, a Black and Jewish interracial couple, found a place Patti and I may have chosen, had we known of it.

2

EXODUS AND EXODUSTERS, PROMISES OF A SHELTERING PLACE

Every spring during the Passover festival, Jews retell the story of the Israelites' escape from slavery. Each year we take the opportunity to tell the story in a different way, and as we age, each time we tell or hear the story it has different meanings. I've known Jews who read the Exodus story as our people's own history. For others, the story is a metaphor for God's relationship to humans or for the way God interacts with history. The stories are about home, exile, sovereignty, responsibility, eternity.

The Exodus story could be rooted in historical facts, or it could be a fable, an allegory, or a spiritual journey written with moral or political purpose. It can be read as a story that happened thousands of years ago or that happened 150 years ago, is happening now, or hasn't happened yet. It could be a constitution for a patriarchy, as the Israeli feminist Esther

Fuchs writes in *Sexual Politics in the Biblical Narrative.* Or it could be a blueprint for liberation.

I wonder: Whose story is it that is told in the Torah? Is the cycle of slavery and liberation unending? Do we recreate the cycle by retelling it every year? Is the cycle a spiral moving toward something better? For many years, because the patriarchal stories told in the Bible were a hindrance to imagining and creating a new, nonhierarchical paradigm, I tried to leave the whole biblical text behind, but I couldn't do it.

A central part of the Passover ritual asks Jews to imagine ourselves into the story of the Exodus. We say, "We were slaves to Pharaoh in Egypt / *avodim hayinu l'paroh b'mitzraim.*" Jews not only try to feel our way into the ancient story but also think about current ways that we are enslaved: social, economic, psychological "narrow places / *mitzraim.*"

For the past couple of decades, my seder table has included Jews who consider themselves to be descendants of people enslaved 2,500 years ago in Egypt, and also Jews and non-Jews whose people were enslaved almost within living memory, including my spouse and our two daughters. As our daughters grew, our family told the story of the journey to freedom in ways that we thought were appropriate to the girls' ages, and also in ways that brought in contemporary issues of persecution and injustice.

At a seder not long ago, with friends and family, including my then-teenage daughters, we conducted the ritual storytelling by letting each person at the table tell a part of the story in their own way. I read a favorite children's book about the Exodus told from the point of view of a young Israelite child. One of my daughters was the only one who brought a contemporary issue to the table: violence among teenage girls. Later, she told me the whole evening felt uncomfortable to her—that white Jews focusing on slavery 2,500 years ago felt to her like white privilege, a ritual that excluded rather than included her. I didn't know at the time how much she longed for the words to speak to her, but her challenge deeply affected me and drove me to dig deeper into the meanings of the biblical Exodus story for American descendants of enslaved Africans.

In his introduction to the anthology *African Americans and the Bible*, Vincent Wimbush writes that for African Americans, "It [the Bible] quickly came to function as a language-world, the storehouse of rhetorics, images, and stories that, through a complex history of engagement, helped establish African Americans as a circle of the biblical imaginary. It helped them imagine themselves as something other, in another world, different from what their immediate situation reflected or demanded."

Wimbush's words shifted my world, allowing me—an Ashkenazi Jewish woman living in the United States and coded as white—to decenter my relationship to the Exodus story. My Jewish practice taught me to ground my sense of self by ritually imagining myself in the Exodus story. Enslaved Africans, I am beginning to understand, used the story to imagine themselves into—to create—freedom, something that they did not actually experience in their lifetimes. For Jews and enslaved Africans, being free has included searching for a place, a land, or a connection to God through which to experience freedom.

The man my Aunt Rose married, Zebedee Arnwine, was born in Cherokee County in East Texas. The county had been named for the Native Americans who, in the 1820s, walked from what we call western North Carolina through Tennessee, Missouri, and Arkansas, and who settled where they found rivers and streams, rolling hills of pine and hardwood forests with a humid, subtropical climate. The region had been home for centuries to the complex, ritual mound-building Caddo civilization. In *Peace Came in the Form of a Woman: Indians and Spaniards in the Texas Borderlands*, Juliana Barr estimates that in 1520, when the Spaniards entered this same area, 250,000 Caddo individuals were living there in small villages. The majority of the Caddo died from diseases brought by the Europeans. With less than 10 percent of their people surviving, the Caddo were pushed out of their lands, west and north into Oklahoma, where the Caddo Nation now lives.

At the same time in the 1820s that the Cherokee came to East Texas, the newly independent Mexican government was marketing the land for Anglo settlement, and, too, African people escaping slavery were arriving in the area, traveling on native trails through Mississippi, Arkansas, and Louisiana. The trickle of African Americans slowly increased, especially after 1829, when the Mexican government abolished slavery.

However, just seven years later, in 1836, the newly independent Republic of Texas legalized slavery as its very first piece of legislation. The Texan legislature wanted to entice new settlement by white Southern plantation owners, people like Albartis Arnwine, Zebedee Arnwine's white forebear, who had been living in Tennessee. In 1840, Albartis relocated himself and the people he owned to the Republic of Texas and settled in what would come to be called

Cherokee County. Zebedee Arnwine's ancestor, perhaps his great grandfather, Cal, was born in 1839 to Mary, a woman Albartis bought just as he was setting out for Texas.

While Albartis Arnwine had plenty of land, the business that he ran was a corn grist mill. In 1850, when Albartis was running his grist mill in Cherokee County and alienating himself from his white neighbors by sharing his home with Gracie, who was also his slave, there were 454 farms in Cherokee County, mostly small homesteads of forty acres or so. Few of the homesteaders owned enslaved people. In 1850, Albartis Arnwine was among the exceptions, but not for long. By 1860 and the beginning of the Civil War, several plantation owners from Mississippi and Louisiana had moved into Cherokee County, bringing the enslaved people they owned.

As the county became filled, Albartis Arnwine went against the grain again: In 1855, he arranged in his will for the manumission of all the twenty-one people he owned, which included Cal, the man that could be Zebedee Arnwine's great-grandfather. However, there was an immediate problem that prevented them from being freed: Albartis's brothers and other white heirs contested the will. The legal battle over Albartis's will, which rose all the way to the Texas Supreme Court and was decided in 1859, involved the will's provision that the newly freed people had to be relocated out of Texas.

The Texas state constitution prohibited free Black people from living in Texas without special permission, and it denied citizenship rights to the few free Black people who lived in the state. Albartis's will instructed his executors to sell his land and use the proceeds to relocate the newly freed families. The executors took control of the property but did not help relocate the families living there. The Texas Supreme Court decided that the provisions in Albartis's will should be implemented, but the American Civil War and the Emancipation Proclamation made the court's decision irrelevant. The Arnwines stayed in Texas after the Civil War, though the land they had lived on and developed for decades had already been stolen.

The youngest of the people Albartis had owned, Sterling Arnwine, who was eighteen months old when Albartis died, was interviewed some ninety odd years later, and his words have been preserved among 2,300 other interviews of ex-slaves in the monumental *Born in Slavery: Slave Narratives from the Federal Writers' Project, 1936 to 1938*. Sterling described what happened like this:

> Massa Arnwine died 'fore de war and he made a will and it gave all he owned to the women he owned, and Jedge Jowell promised massa on his deathbed he would take us to de free country, but he didn't. He took us to his place to work for him for 'bout two years and the women never did get that 900 acres of land Massa Arnwine willed to 'em. I don't know who got it, but they didn't.

Albartis's will is not mentioned in *Cherokee County History*, an official book on the county's history, but in the book's chapter on Jacksonville, Cherokee County's principal city, this story is recorded:

> When the Southern states began seceding from the Union in 1860, and before Texas had made an official decision,

> Jacksonville citizens staged their own secession celebration by gathering in the town square to raise the Texas flag. Just before the flag reached the top of the 75-foot pole the rope broke and the flag fluttered down, much to the crowd's dismay. Climbing the pole to attach a new rope defied all attempts until Calhoun Arnwine, a young, free black man, made the ascent and saved the day.

In 1860, Cal would have been about twenty-one. Throughout most of the prior five years, he, his mother Mary, and several other Arnwine families had been in legal limbo, denied their promised freedom. Yet right before the Texas flag raising, the Texas Supreme Court ruled to support Albartis's will, which affirmed the Arnwines' freedom only if they were relocated out of Texas. Cal and his family stayed in Texas, and forty years later his descendant Zebedee was born in Jacksonville. After the Civil War, newly freed African Americans founded dozens of all-Black towns in eastern Texas. Among the towns was Weeping Mary, a community two sisters who had been born into slavery began when they purchased plots of land on what had been the heart of the Caddo people's civilization.

The foregrounded origin of the name Weeping Mary is a reference to Mary Magdalene weeping at Jesus's grave, but local folklore conveys other stories. Variations of a local legend tells the story of a Black woman named Mary weeping inconsolably from the devastating loss of her land to a white man.

The biblical imaginary that Vincent Wimbush wrote about in *African Americans and the Bible* mirrored reality, as promises made, left unfulfilled, and then revoked by the post-Reconstruction government were not unlike the biblical Egyptian pharaoh's wavering negotiations with Moses. The Mississippi River, like the Red Sea and the Jordan River, needed to be crossed for the formerly enslaved to find freedom.

The Southern Homestead Act of 1866 proposed to open up 44 million acres of land in the South to African American freedmen and whites who had been loyal to the Union. This seemingly abundant amount of land turned out to be undesirable as farmland, difficult to cultivate, especially without the resources needed to start a homestead. In the end, only about one thousand African American families were able to fulfill the requirements to claim permanent deeds to the eighty-acre plots in the South. The vast majority of freed people experienced only the disappointment of an unfulfilled promise. In 1877, twelve years after the Civil War and fourteen after the Emancipation Proclamation, white Southerners were defiantly talking about a return to the slave system and Southern Black people were convinced a return to chattel slavery was just around the corner.

This is the era when the term *bulldozer* was coined to refer to the white Democratic Party enforcers who brutalized and humiliated African Americans who attempted to run for political office or even tried to vote. This is the way the origin of the expression *bulldozer* was explained in the *Gettysburg Compiler* on January 11, 1877:

> In very obstinate cases the brethren [white men] were in the habit of administering a "bull's dose" of several hundred lashes on the bare back. When dealing with those who were hard to convert, active members would call out "give

> me the whip and let me give him a bull-dose." From this it became easy to say "that fellow ought to be bull-dosed, or bull-dozed," and soon bull-doze, bull-dozing and bull-dozers came to be slang words.

The end of Reconstruction gave sanction to unbridled brutality and restriction on movement, commerce, and political agency for African Americans living in the South. Vagrancy laws limited movement and voting laws limited political involvement. Bulldozers attacked local leaders. The idea that African Americans must leave the South in order to survive took hold and spread as quickly as if the internet already existed.

Nell Irvin Painter's book *Exodusters: Black Migration to Kansas After Reconstruction* tells the story of the migration of freed people who, after Reconstruction ended in 1877, rushed to leave the intolerable conditions in the South. They aimed to move to Kansas to seek the lives emancipation had allowed them to imagine. In her introduction, Painter writes that land was the first and foremost goal of freed people in the South. For freed people, acquiring land meant owning the means to support their families, the fulfilment of freedom.

The Civil Rights Act of 1875, the last Reconstruction Era piece of legislation, required equal treatment in public accommodations and transportation. The act was never enforced, but in the hope that the steamboats traveling up the river would comply with the law, freed people saved up their fare, packed everything they could carry, camped on both the Mississippi and Louisiana shores of the Mississippi River, and frantically signaled to the boats to pick them up. Painter describes the scene as desperate and chaotic, yet purposeful and imbued with full faith that once they were across the river—in other words, made it out of the South to St. Louis—God would provide the ways and means to make it to the Promised Land of Kansas.

When the exodusters reached St. Louis, they encountered a segregated but growing city that would be changed by their presence. Black churches and newly formed Black civic groups raised money to feed and house the travelers and send them on their way. Black community leaders formed the St. Louis Colored Relief Board, and it grew to include twenty-five of the city's prominent Black clergypersons, businesspeople, and professionals, and to raise several thousand dollars almost entirely from the Black community. White officials were afraid that if the exodusters were given aid, they would continue to come. The truth was that the exodusters would continue to come whether they received aid or not. It was the intolerable conditions in the South—and their faith that freedom was possible—that drove them.

Exoduster is a peculiarly American word, with connections literal and obvious to the story told in the Torah of the Israelites' exodus from Egypt, while the *-ster* suffix is tied to American slang—songster, hipster, roadster, and so on—making it sound adventurous and offbeat. *Dust*, meanwhile, invokes the journey to Kansas: hot, dry, and exhausting. *Exoduster* is a word that knots together Jewish and African American stories, from before my Aunt Rose and Mr. Arnwine tangled their lives together, and well before Patti, the girls, and I wove together our Black and Jewish family.

Black culture and politics in St. Louis were deeply affected by the 1877 influx of African Americans from the South, by the support they received from the African American community, and by the hostility from the white power structure. In 1892, my great-grandparents Mordche and Zlate Kinberg and their young sons Mendel (who became Max) and eight-year-old Yosef (who became Joseph) immigrated to St. Louis. The young Kinberg family had come from the Kremenets district of the Russian Empire, an area that is now Ukraine. They lived so close to what was then the Austro-Hungarian (now Polish) border that a Jew could walk across to escape to relative freedom. In St. Louis, the Kinbergs found a city shaped by the racial segregation experienced by the exodusters. The adjacent Black and Jewish tenement neighborhoods where my grandfather Joseph grew up and married—where my father and Aunt Rose were born—were filled with immigrants and exodusters.

The first years of the twentieth century were restless for the Kinbergs and for the Arnwines, too. My great-grandmother Zlata (who became Laura in America) died in childbirth in 1897 while giving birth to her sixth child. Two children had died before the family left Eastern Europe. My grandfather Joseph, her oldest-living child, was a teenager when she passed, and he tried living in Chicago for a while before returning to St. Louis and marrying my grandmother Yetta (who became Ethel). They had their first child, my Aunt Laura, in 1906.

Zebedee Arnwine was born around the turn of the century. Soon after his birth in East Texas in 1902, Zebedee's parents moved their family three hundred miles straight north to Indian Territory, to what would become, in 1907, the state of Oklahoma. The Arnwine family's move to the area near Muskogee, Oklahoma, was part of a large migration of Black farmers, a wave that came a generation after the exodusters of 1877 yet before the Great Migration to the North. This relocation included thousands of families who organized all-Black towns in a part of the Indian Territory where some were advocating for an all-Black state. They were dreaming of a place where Black people could live free from ever-present degradations and violence.

My nineteen-year-old daughter came into my bedroom one night not long after George Floyd was murdered to tell me about a TikTok she'd just viewed of a white supremacist angrily ranting about an all-Black town somewhere in the South.

"I want to go live in that town," my daughter said. She didn't know that I was writing, just then, about all-Black towns in Oklahoma three generations ago. I see in her generation the same deep desire to be free from ever-present racism.

Living with and loving my daughter, I feel the sharp contours of her broken heart: The women she feels most secure with, her white-appearing mothers, occupy the same class as people who might decide to take her life at any time. I remember the moment she came home from school, at six years old, having just learned that Dr. Martin Luther King Jr., the man every white person around her lauded and admired, had been assassinated by a white man. This fact so unmoored her, she had trouble going to school during January and February for the next twelve years. She knew she would be reminded of the assassination. I am not surprised she wants to live in an all-Black town, feeling, as I often have, my inadequacy to comfort and protect her. In *Acres of Aspiration: The All-Black Towns in Oklahoma*, Hannibal B. Johnson explains:

> Beyond the natural yearning for freedom, many Blacks held firm to a perceived economic truth: land ownership held the key to success. Moreover, they thought land ownership would lead inexorably to full citizenship. . . . In trickles, then in torrents, Blacks streamed first into Kansas, then increasingly into Oklahoma. This bold swim upstream by Black pioneers sparked controversy, then fear and resentment, among local whites. This decidedly mixed reception failed to stem the tide of migrants. The floodgates having parted, a cascade of newcomers spilled across the region. Oklahoma, some thought, would evolve into an all-Black state captained by a Black governor. All-Black towns and settlements in the windswept Oklahoma plains captured the collective imagination of an entire people.

While some were imagining an all-Black state in the Indian Territory, the US federal government adopted bureaucratic, legal mechanisms to allot Native American tribal lands to individuals who could be proven to be members of the Choctaw, Chickasaw, Muscogee, Cherokee, or Seminole tribes. In 1887, the Dawes Act authorized the US president to subdivide communal tribal lands into individual allotments. Nine years later, in 1898, the Curtis Amendment to the Dawes Act abolished tribal governments and assigned the Dawes Commission the responsibility of determining each individual's tribal membership. The racial and economic struggles in the Indian Territory during those years were unique, in part because the Black slaves of some of the tribes, freed by the Civil War, were also considered tribal members and could be included in the allotments. Known as the "Creek Freedmen," the people enslaved by members of the Creek tribe, and the descendants of these enslaved individuals, had complicated relationships with African Americans arriving from other parts of the South.

Zebedee Arnwine was perhaps five years old when the Indian and Oklahoma Territories became the state of Oklahoma and adopted a Jim Crow constitution. The new state's constitution defined "white race" as everyone except those who were of African descent. It then went on to establish segregated schools and empowered the legislature to limit the voting rights of Black people. The first bill to come before the new Oklahoma Senate established into law the segregation of Black people in public transportation and public facilities.

Just ten years after Oklahoma statehood, Zebedee was working as a farmer with his father when on April 2, 1917, President Woodrow Wilson declared the United States was sending troops to Europe to fight in what would come to be known as World War I because "the world must be made safe for democracy." About a year later, sixteen-year-old Zebedee, claiming he was eighteen, briefly married and registered for the draft. He was one of the several hundred thousand Black men who registered but were not called up.

Tamah, the woman who became Zebedee's second wife (he'd had a short-lived teenage marriage), was born in 1901 to Rebecca Walker, an enrolled Creek Freedman. Still, Rebecca was required to go in person and with a witness before the Dawes Commission in Muskogee, Oklahoma, to enroll three-year-old Tamah into the tribe. A transcript of the Dawes Commission's interview before a panel of white men is preserved in the Oklahoma Historical Society's archives. Enrolling her young daughter into the tribe meant young Tamah would be entitled to an allotment of land in the Muskogee area, in Indian Territory. There was oil and gas under that land. The discovery of oil and gas in the Oklahoma Territory in 1897 (by statehood in 1907, Oklahoma was the largest oil-producing state in the country) fueled the urgency for Native Americans and Creek Freedmen to claim their allotments.

When Tamah was a teenager, her land was leased to an oil and gas company that sent her a monthly check. However, as was common at the time, a white "guardian" was established by the court. The *Muskogee Cimeter*, a local Black newspaper, found more than three thousand similar guardianship cases, showing that $100 million had been stolen from Native American and Black families. In Tamah's case, her appointed guardian was evidently temporary, and he spent a good deal of time in court in an effort to become a permanent guardian by proving Tamah's incompetence to manage her estate. These court proceedings, too, are preserved in the Oklahoma Historical Society library. After three years of legal wrangling, Tamah, when she turned eighteen, won the right to manage her own affairs. Not long after, in January 1921, Tamah married Zebedee Arnwine, and in 1924 they had a daughter they named Rebecca, after Tamah's mother.

Six months into Tamah and Mr. Arnwine's marriage, in June 1921, the Black community of Greenwood, not an hour away from Muskogee, was attacked by a white mob, killing dozens if not hundreds, burning several square blocks, and leaving ten thousand Black people homeless.

Greenwood had been a prosperous Black district within the city of Tulsa with its own thriving economy, professionals, shops, and banks. Tulsa was considered the oil capital of the world, and Greenwood the Black Wall Street.

One eyewitness account of the coordinated destruction of Greenwood was recorded by attorney Buck Colbert Franklin in his autobiography, edited by his son and grandson, historians John Hope and John Whittington Franklin. On the evening of May 31, 1921, Buck Franklin got wind of impending violence, and because he knew so many of Tulsa's leaders, white and Black, he thought he could do something to prevent it:

> I tried to reach [the sheriff's office] but was unsuccessful, and I learned that the [phone] wires were cut. At daybreak [on June 1, 1921] I went to my office still believing I could get to the sheriff's office. But I saw I was too late. Hundreds of men with drawn guns were approaching from every direction. . . . I stood at the steps to my office, and I was immediately arrested and taken to one of the many detention camps. Even then, airplanes were circling overhead, dropping explosives upon the buildings that had been looted, and big trucks were hauling all sorts of furniture and household goods away. In these camps I saw pregnant women, and one was so heavy that a doctor was called in to deliver her baby. Soon I was back upon the streets, but the building where I had my office was a smoldering ruin, and all my lawbooks and office fixtures had been consumed by flames. I went to where my rooming house had stood

> a few short hours before, but it was in ashes, with all my clothes and the money to be used in moving my family. As far as one could see, not a Negro dwelling house or place of business stood.

Buck Franklin describes the trigger to the Tulsa massacre as an accusation against a teenage son of a well-known and respected Greenwood businessman: "The boy was on his job [as a shoe shiner and janitor] and, boarding a very crowded elevator, he accidentally stepped on the lady's foot. She became angry and slapped him, and a fresh, cub newspaper reporter, without any experience and no doubt anxious for a byline, gave out an erroneous report that a Negro had assaulted a white girl."

Familiar-yet-false accusations from white people that Black men commonly attack white women led the way to the Tulsa massacre and to generational trauma still felt today. For instance, in 2018, Charles Blow, a *New York Times* opinion writer, interviewed 103-year-old Olivia J. Hooker, another eyewitness to the Tulsa massacre. Hooker's father owned an upscale department store in 1921, and the family lived in a comfortable five-room home. "White men broke into their house as Hooker and some of her siblings hid beneath an oak dining table, draped with a tablecloth. 'They took a hatchet to my sisters' piano. They poured oil all over my grandmother's bed. They stuffed the dresser with ammunition,' Hooker told me. . . . They broke the phonograph and the Enrico Caruso records her mother had received as a gift from a friend who had gone to study in Heidelberg, Germany."

I can only imagine the effects of this racist violence on young Zebedee Arnwine, despite being witness to my daughters' emerging identities as young Black women. Their self-love and self-doubts, their righteous anger, their rising independence, their bold confrontations—all of these qualities developed amid looping replays of white police beating, strangling, and shooting Black people. My daughters share with me their feelings of anger and vulnerability; because I am white, I know I don't fully feel what they are experiencing. Yet when there was a shooting in a synagogue in Poway, California, and when a rabbi's houseguests were attacked with a machete in Monsey, New York, my daughters were the first to check in with me. We are each familiar with navigating threats of violence, but none of it is simple. I've learned from my nonsimple family how each of us creates our own path through the perils.

3

ROSE'S LIFE IN ST. LOUIS

My grandparents Joseph Kinberg and Yetta Schwartz married in 1905 in a crowded, racially segregated tenement neighborhood. As I imagine and write my Aunt Rose's life, my grandmother, too, is coming alive within me. Both Aunt Rose's life and my grandmother's life are for me a series of frescos, rising in relief beneath my own life in progress, changing the shape even of my memories. I feel their memories rise as well, as if they are my own.

Naming children for relatives who have died is a tradition among Ashkenazi Jews. Perhaps this tradition has aided our survival, making us just a little more conscious of what we carry. Our names are prompts: Who was this person I was named for? Over many generations, our lives and those of our namesakes may blur. For instance, it is possible that the biblical Abraham of the Torah was many generations of Abrahams, with all of their stories told as if they belonged to one person. Perhaps, in the distant future, the story of my life, the people I am named for, and my future namesakes will be told as one adventurous journey.

My given name, Clarette, is a combination of Clara, for an aunt of my mother, and Yetta, for my paternal grandmother—Aunt Rose's mother—who died in 1951, four years before I was born. I wish I could remember asking my father, even once, about his—and Aunt Rose's—mother.

The Romanian Jews of my grandmother's generation were stateless. The Romanian Constitution adopted in 1866, only one year after the end of the American Civil War, stipulated that only "members of the Christian rite" could be citizens, making permanent foreigners of the hundreds of thousands of Jews who lived in the nation, and catalyzing decades of increasingly antisemitic laws and restrictions.

Jews had lived in Romania for centuries before this constitution was written. They had lived in their own communities, developing their own language and culture, and at the same time had become acculturated into Romanian life. However, after the 1866 constitution, they were pushed further into the margins, denied even the separate spaces they had carved out for themselves. Jews could not own or cultivate land or travel to peddle goods. Jews could not become officers in the military, customs officials, journalists, craftspeople, or clerks. Anti-Jewish laws were scaffolded on age-old lies related to Jews poisoning Christians, Jewish immorality and licentiousness, and Jewish untrustworthiness. Jews could not vote or obtain licenses to sell alcohol. Jews could not own or manage pharmacies. Jews could not sell tobacco or soda water or certain baked goods. Fewer than 10 percent of Jewish children were allowed to attend public schools, and Jews were prohibited from opening their own schools.

In 1899–1900, several anti-Jewish riots broke out, and there was a violent pogrom in Iași: "For several hours there was fighting, merciless blows, pillaging, and devastation, all under the paternal eyes of the police authorities and the army, which interfered only to hinder the Jews from defending themselves," reported the *American Jewish Yearbook* in 1900. Three years later, the Kishinev pogrom, during which forty-nine Jews were murdered, hundreds of women raped, and homes and businesses destroyed, was reported around the world.

Young Jews of Romania told their parents they were leaving, walking out of Romania. The *fusgeyers* (a Yiddish word meaning "walking wayfarers") packed what they could carry and formed groups to walk from Romania through Hungary, Austria, Germany, and the Netherlands to catch boats to North America. Along the way, they organized groups, stopped and gave speeches, put on plays, and asked for donations to continue their journey. They had to cross the Carpathian Mountains and walk through dangerous countryside where those considered foreigners and strangers were sometimes hunted down. For instance, there were bounties on Romani travelers, and shooting homeless and stateless Jews could be done without a second thought. The *fusgeyer* movement, beginning in 1899 and lasting almost to World War I (1914), was a young people's solution to living in a country where they could not be citizens, where they were reviled, and where, after the pogroms in the Romanian city of Iași and the Russian city of Kishinev, they feared for their lives. Perhaps my grandmother, Aunt Rose's mother, was among the *fusgeyers*, taking her future into her own hands and feet, and walking from her home in Romania to a port in Amsterdam. Did sixteen-year-old Yetta Schwartz walk or ride in a wagon or train from her home in Romania to Antwerp, Belgium, to board the boat that would take her to the United States?

When she arrived in New York from Romania in November 1903, traveling without any family, she had a note with the address of a relative who lived in a St. Louis rooming house with other recent immigrants. She was among hundreds of Romanian Jews arriving weekly. Like Yetta, most of them rarely spoke of the Romania they left behind. As far as I can tell, no one in my family knows any particulars of Yetta's life in the old country. Perhaps Aunt Rose did—if only I could ask.

Yetta Schwartz might have been born in Iași, about eighty miles west of the Russian (now Ukrainian) town of Kishinev, where the pogrom during the year Yetta left her home shook the Jewish world. In 1899, there were close to forty thousand Jews living in Iași, where, I read in an encyclopedia, Jewish culture was strongly influenced by Hasidism.

Perhaps Yetta grew up farther north in the farming hub of Botoșani, which in 1900 had the third-largest Jewish community in Romania, and where, according to Romanian genealogists, Schwartz was the third most common surname. On a day trip from Botoșani, you could walk north to the Ukrainian shtetl of Khotin, where Sephardic Jews had settled and formed a mercantile link to the larger city of Lviv another few days' walk north. Just a little farther, you might pass by Pochaiv, the birth shtetl of Joseph Kinberg, Yetta's eventual husband.

Of course, Yetta could have been from Bucharest, Romania's cosmopolitan capital, its largest city, and home to a fast-growing Jewish community in 1900.

I have a memory of a conversation with a family member about our Romanian roots. It might have been a dream, or I could have imagined it altogether. In the memory, I ask, "Where in Romania did Grandma come from?" And with a flourish to show off my tiny bit of geographic knowledge, I add, "Was it Bucharest?" The answer, from a person I cannot draw up in memory—perhaps my father, or an aunt or uncle—with an inscrutable gleam of surprise and an equally opaque sense of relief, replies, "Yes, yes, Bucharest, yes, Bucharest."

This answer, the triple affirmative, made me doubt the surety of Bucharest. All at once, there seemed to be more to the story. "Yes, yes, Bucharest" merely affirmed a satisfactory answer to the question of Grandma's hometown, with my family member relieved that no more need be said, because no more could be said. Nothing more is known. All of the documentation of Yetta Schwartz's life, decades of census forms, and the final death certificate claim Romania as her birthplace, with nothing more specific.

So little was known about Yetta's background even within the family that her daughter Rose didn't know Yetta's maiden name.

When my father's oldest sister, Laura—born in 1907, just a year before Aunt Rose—began conversations with me, she often said, "*Farshteystu* Yiddish? Do you understand Yiddish? Ach, no, of course not." Sometimes she even said, "*Farshteystu* Jewish?" She used the Yiddish word for *understand* and the English word for *Yiddish*. Through this ritual, Aunt Laura communicated to me that Jewishness was central to us both, yet at the same time, these conversations made clear that she questioned whether I could understand the basics of our shared identity. The world she'd grown up in had faded; the desire to pass something on remained, but we did not share the language she wished to use to do so. Neither the everydayness of Yiddish nor the language of prayer was passed down to me.

If I could ask Aunt Rose now to tell me about her early life, I imagine she would begin, "*Farshteystu* Yiddish? That's okay, I don't either anymore. But Yiddish is the only language Mama spoke to us—Laura, Tillie, Morrie, Harry, Gertie, and me. When baby Leonard was born in 1922, I was fourteen, and by the time he could talk, I was rarely home." The Kinbergs spoke Yiddish at home because Yiddish would have been the only language my grandparents—she from Romania, he from Russia (what is now Ukraine)—could converse in.

According to the 1910 and 1920 censuses and my grandfather's death certificate in 1925, my grandfather's occupation was junk dealer. I'm familiar with what a junk dealer does because my father carried on in the business. A junk dealer buys and sells scrap metal or other pieces and parts of used machinery. Selling metal parts passed from father to son. My grandfather might have kept his junk in a yard vault underneath the family's rear apartment at 1418 1/2 North Tenth Street in St. Louis, which at that time was a tenement district with dilapidated, overcrowded, and unsanitary conditions, as recorded in detail in a Civic League of St. Louis report written the year Aunt Rose was born, 1908. In their house-by-house survey, the civic league found, for instance, that 93 percent of surveyed families did not have a toilet in their apartment. Instead, occupants used shared privy vaults in the backyard next to the storage vaults where I imagine my grandfather's junk was kept. Ninety-six percent of the families did not have access to a bathtub; there was one public bath in the area.

The forty-eight-block area under study in the report had the worst conditions in the city. Thirteen thousand people, categorized by the report as comprising 30 percent Jews, 30 percent Italians, 15 percent Negroes, and 25 percent Poles and other nationalities, lived in the area the civic league studied. A close look at the 1910 census—which includes Joseph and Yetta Kinberg and their three young daughters, Laura, Rose, and Tillie—shows that each ethnic group lived in clusters, the adjoining blocks of ethnically segregated families all living in the same terrible conditions.

The Kinbergs' 1910 census page included four coal miners; a tobacco stemmer; several laborers working on the railroad, in a steel foundry, and in a lumberyard; two bricklayers; and two cabinetmakers—all coded as white. Joseph Kinberg, the junk dealer, was the only person on the page that had his own business. While only a handful of the neighborhood Jews were listed as born in the United States, Yetta Kinberg was the only one listed from Romania.

Ten years later, by the time of the 1920 census, the family had moved eight blocks directly west, farther from the river, to the Kerry Patch, a neighborhood of Jews and Irish Catholics.

I have a photo of my father and four of his siblings in the Kerry Patch years. They are sitting on the hard scrabble of what is likely their front yard at 1718 O'Fallon Street in a part of North St. Louis that will be razed in the decades to come, making way for a series of urban renewal fiascos doomed by poverty and racist city policy. In the background, about half a block away, is the Kregel Casket Company building on the corner of North Eighteenth and O'Fallon.

The large-nosed, squinting boy in the beanie is no doubt my father, Morrie. My father had a self-conscious perception that he had an oversize nose. One of his favorite lines: "When God was handing out noses, I thought he said 'roses,' so I asked for a big red one." I don't remember my father ever mentioning God in another context.

Sometimes I can't stop looking at this photo of the five siblings. Aunt Gertie, the youngest in the photo, is sitting cross-legged in the front. Harry, just a year younger than my father, is on the left. Laura, the oldest, is behind my father and Gertie. The girl on the right could be either my Aunt Rose or Tillie. There is no longer anyone alive who can confirm who it is. Like the casket and funeral supplies company in the background, death and separation loom for this quintet.

The first picture I was able to locate that I knew included Aunt Rose—because it was labeled on the back—was in a photo album belonging to Rose's sister, my Aunt Laura. After Laura passed away in 1995, her photo albums were passed on to her great-granddaughter, also named Laura, my first cousin twice removed.

My Aunt Rose's brief first marriage at age seventeen was to an Ashkenazi Jewish man, Edward O., who was seven years older than her. They had a son, Joey, in 1927, and divorced when Joey was a baby. According to family lore, Edward had an affair with a nurse in the hospital while Aunt Rose was in labor; according to Joey's adoption papers,

An undated photo of Aunt Rose, sometime in the 1920s, found in her sister Laura's photo album long after both had died.

both Aunt Rose and Edward abandoned Joey on the date of their divorce in 1928. Joey was placed in the St. Louis Jewish Orphan's Home and then cared for by Rose's mother until his official adoption at age eleven, in 1939, by Rose's sister Gertie and her husband Hy.

I have found very little about the family between the years 1928 and 1933, other than that Joey was moved around between various family members and the Jewish Orphan's Home and that, by 1933, Aunt Rose was living separately and some of her younger siblings were forbidden to talk to her. I've imagined Aunt Rose telling me the story from her point of view.

By 1925, we had moved to 5050 Cates, right off Kingshighway, to a two-story house, nicer than anything we'd had before, but things turned sour right away. In April, Zaydeh Max, my father's father, died suddenly of an aortic aneurism. He had been living in Toledo for a long while, but when his second wife died, he moved back to St. Louis. A few months later, I married Eddie, that good-looking mamzer, I was just seventeen years old, and he was twenty-four. The very next day, August 17, 1925, Papa had a stroke and died. He was in the ground before we even knew what had happened.

There were seven of us kids. Laura was eighteen, and baby Leonard was just three. Mama still didn't speak English, even though she'd been in America for twenty-one years. I just remember the vacant stare, the rigid demands. Mama said my marriage to Eddie caused Papa's stroke, and the rest of them thought so too—or, anyway, took Mama's side against me. I could hear them asking me, "What else could have killed him the day after Rabbi Goldenson signed the paper?"

Eddie never moved in, and I never moved out, but I got pregnant anyway. And then my brother Harry died. His death changed everything. Everyone was just sad all the time. Two months later, on September 20, 1927, my son was born. Of course, I named him Joseph after my father. Everyone called him Joey.

Eddie was on the move all the time, selling shmatas *out of the trunk of his car. His family had a store selling this and that, and they sent him on the road with samples: Kansas City, Oklahoma, Texas. He was never a father to Joey. While I lay in the hospital, nineteen years old, Eddie was out in the halls flirting with the nurses. After Joey was born, Eddie wanted nothing to do with us, and I wanted nothing to do with him either. I was already being shunned by the family, who blamed Papa's death on me because of my marriage to Eddie.*

When Eddie and I divorced, Joey wasn't even walking yet. I was terrified by the thought that I couldn't care for little Joey—that the house might not be safe for children because of whatever unknown danger had caused Harry's death. My little brother Leonard was just six years old. Harry got sick first with chest pain, and then suddenly he couldn't breathe. It felt so abrupt, but maybe we just hadn't been paying attention.

After Harry died, Laura and Morrie acted as though they couldn't stand to look at me, pregnant and confused. Tillie, meanwhile, started crying the day Papa died and never stopped.

Morrie and Laura, and Mama, kept complaining about the baby being a burden, and I had nowhere to go with Joey, so I brought him to the Jewish Orphan's Home. Finally, my mother relented and said she would care for him. I moved out with some other girls, and although I lived around the corner from the family, I stayed away as much as possible. Joey became part of my mother's family. The family that had once been mine but had slipped away. I was on my own.

I know Joey can never forgive me. I left him. I abandoned him. As a baby, Joey had the face of an angel. But I couldn't stay there to raise him, and I couldn't take him with me. Or maybe I could have. I'll never know, and neither will he. The Great Depression began years early for us, in 1925, when Papa died, when Harry died, when my disastrous marriage with Eddie began and quickly collapsed, when the debate over who would take care of Joey became an uproar.

When my baby sister Gertie married Hy, Joey moved in with them; he was seven years old and finally had a place in the family. By that time, Eddie had remarried and moved with the new wife to Muskogee. When Gertie and Hy's lawyer sent him a letter about their plan to adopt Joey, I doubt Eddie even read it. Gertie had been a kid, just twelve, when I had Joey, and she fell in love with him immediately. When he was a baby, she pretended to be his mother. When I took him to the Jewish Orphan's Home, she threw a fit like we'd never seen. After she married Hy, she got to be his mother. Even before I took up with Zeb, they tried to cut me off. The way they treated me, it hurt. I felt like they just wanted me to go away.

I was still in my twenties and on my own. I needed a job, but in our family, we only worked for ourselves. We were peddlers and junk dealers. Any money we made was used to buy something we could sell. If someone in the family got a little extra money, they became a jobber, like Uncle Jack, my father's younger brother and the only one of us who had two nickels to rub together. A jobber didn't sell any particular thing. They just looked for a bunch of something to buy straight from anyone who wanted to unload it. Then the jobber found someone else who wanted it.

The house at 5050 Cates, where my grandfather died in 1925. Photo taken in 2016.

In our neighborhood, everyone wanted to be a jobber. A jobber had something. Top of the line was opening a storefront, like Uncle Jack. In 1921, he opened Kinberg Hardware on Franklin Avenue. Mostly, he sold paint, so he was a paint jobber.

I worked in the store for a while, and so did my brother Morrie, but that wasn't good because we weren't on speaking terms. So I made the rounds of the department stores: Stix, Famous, Barneys, Vandevoorts, Scruggs. Finally, I got on at Woolworth's five-and-dime when they opened the store on Franklin, not far from Kinberg Hardware.

The week I started at Woolworth's, the colored girls threw up a picket. I had to walk right through them to get in the door, but I did stop to read the signs: "Don't buy where you can't work." It really didn't have anything to do with me: I couldn't buy anything unless I was working, and I was so relieved to have the job at Woolworth's. But the pickets really rubbed Morrie and Jack the wrong way. They wanted to keep to themselves and didn't want to be told who to hire. They didn't want any trouble, and down the street was too close.

I didn't know what to think, but right then, I couldn't be on the same side as Morrie about anything. I started to pay more attention to what the picketers were saying.

Franklin Avenue formed the southern edge of what a decade earlier, in the early 1920s, had been described as the Jewish ghetto, a few dozen blocks of Eastern European immigrant families hemmed in by "No Jews need apply" signs in the apartments farther north and south of the city's center.

Jews who could afford it found that there were pockets of residential housing directly west of the city center where they could move. Movement for Black people was much more severely restricted than for Jews. In 1916, when my Aunt Rose was eight years old, St. Louis voters had passed, by a huge margin, a voter-initiative-based segregation ordinance, the first in the country. White (including some Jewish) precincts that bordered Black neighborhoods voted by a margin of eight to one to make it illegal for Black people to move into white neighborhoods. According to the "Segregation of the Negro Ordinance," no person could move onto a block where 75 percent of that block's inhabitants were of a different race. This ordinance specified "Negro" and "white," yet there was also ambivalence in its language regarding "different" races. This was particularly relevant to

Jews, who were sometimes considered a separate race, not included in the white racial category. Since Jews could often phenotypically pass for white, Jewish people might have to declare their Jewishness for it to be known. The situation had similarities to the 1993 policy on LGBTQ people in the US military referred to as "Don't ask, don't tell." This policy both prohibited queer people from serving in the military and at the same time allowed them to serve as long as they did not reveal this facet of their identity. With racial segregation ordinances, Jews could not know with certainty whether, if their Jewishness were known, the ordinance would restrict them from white neighborhoods.

When the Supreme Court struck down a similar ordinance in Louisville, Kentucky, the next year, however, white people began the practice of attaching "restrictive covenants" to property deeds. This became common practice as a way to continue segregation without breaking the law. Restrictive covenants often specified that both Black people and Jews were prohibited from buying properties, codifying that for real estate contracts, Jews were neither Black nor white.

By the time my father's siblings were old enough to find their own places to live, rising antisemitism was making it harder for Jews to slip under the racial radar, especially in the years after the 1929 stock market crash. In this period, Father Charles Coughlin, a Detroit-based priest with a radio show, began using explosive, inflammatory, and antisemitic rhetoric in his broadcasts: *The financial system has played such an important part in closing factories, in creating unemployment, in confiscating homes, in raising taxes, and in forcing you to eke out an existence from hand to mouth. You have been victimized by an economic system which is unsound, un-Christian, and un-American.*

Tens of millions of people in the United States tuned into Father Coughlin's broadcasts, which increasingly focused on the "money changers in the temple." Father Coughlin promoted the conspiracy theory that Communism was a Jewish plot. He unceasingly railed against this mythic "Judeo-Bolshevism" on his weekly broadcasts. By 1935, his messages had become anti-Roosevelt and nascently pro-Nazi, and irresistible to the white public tuning in both because of Father Coughlin's mastery of radio broadcasting and their contemporary economic hardships begging explanation.

In journalist Andrew Lapin's series of podcasts titled *Radioactive*, which focuses on Father Coughlin, Lapin explains the early reception of Father Coughlin's broadcasts among Jews: "Several of the Detroit Jewish communities' most prominent leaders accepted Father Coughlin's distinction between the good Jews and the bad." In an interview with a Detroit community newspaper, Father Coughlin stated that he was "a friend and champion of the Jewish people," and two of the leading rabbis at the time spoke at the priest's massive rallies. When a prominent Detroit rabbi, Leon Fram, loudly denounced Father Coughlin's rhetoric as bad for the Jews, he was criticized in his community for creating a needless panic.

But ordinary Jews listening in weren't so sure of Father Coughlin either. Father Coughlin frequently repeated the language of Julius Streicher, an organizer of the Nazis' anti-Jewish boycott of April 1933: "*Die Juden sind unser Unglück.*" *Jews are our misfortune.*

Yet on Sunday afternoons, you could hear Father Coughlin's voice on the radios all over the Jewish neighborhoods in St. Louis. According to one person Andrew Lapin spoke to, "My aunt and uncle [in St. Louis] were, of course, outraged, but it also was something they wanted to hear because the accusations sometimes struck close to home and soul. Father Coughlin was a steady diet."

My family, like other Jews in St. Louis, navigated this Depression-era mix of racism and antisemitism with overlapping strategies: They affirmed their identity on the white side of the Black/white racial divide; they moved within residential and social circles that were exclusively Jewish; and they tended to hide their Jewish affiliation during the unfortunate occasions when they found themselves outside of their community.

Each federal census shows my family's westward migration measured in city blocks: From Tenth Street (that is, ten blocks from the Mississippi River) in 1910 to Eighteenth Street in 1920. When my grandfather Joseph Kinberg died in 1927, my family had moved another thirty blocks west, and by 1930 they had moved to the city's western edge.

The 1930 census shows that my Aunt Rose still lived with her mother and her five living siblings, and that she worked as a salesclerk in dry goods. By 1932, though, she was living separately, about a block away from the rest of her family, still squarely in a white, Jewish neighborhood.

I imagine Aunt Rose on her way downtown to work, or looking for work, and as she exits the streetcar on Franklin Avenue, she finds herself in the midst of an event that launched a powerful wave of civil rights activity in St. Louis. Picketers are walking in a wide circle in front of the new

Woolworth's five-and-dime, but they're also in front of the fish store and the dry goods store nearby.

In 1931, when the multinational corporation F. W. Woolworth opened its sixth five-and-dime store in St. Louis, it was picketed by an ad hoc group of African Americans who were fed up with retail stores in their neighborhoods that did not hire Black salesclerks. This particular Woolworth's at 2612 Franklin Avenue was surrounded by shops owned and operated by Jewish families who had lived nearby but had recently moved a few miles west of their stores. Brasch Furniture, Zorensky Brothers ("Home of good clothes, hats, furnishings, and shoes"), and Louis Gelb's fish store were among the new Woolworth's neighbors. Franklin Avenue was lined with dusty two- and three-story brick storefronts extending eastward to Fourteenth Street, where my Great-Uncle Jack's Kinberg Hardware stood. Across the street from the hardware store was the Globe Theatre, which, along with talkies, still advertised vaudeville shows.

Black attorney David Grant describes the decision to picket the new Woolworth's in an oral history.

> In 1931, Woolworth's Dime Store was putting up a store they built in the 2600 block on the south side of the street of Franklin Avenue. They proposed to open that store without a single black clerk. It was then that we got this ad hoc group together . . . called the "Neighborhood Improvement" or some such thing. The *St. Louis ARGUS* [*Newspaper*] printed fifty thousand handbills for us free, with which we circularized the entire area. . . . We went to management and asked them to hire some black clerks, and they said they had black janitors in white stores, so why did we

A protester holds a sign that reads, "Don't buy where you can't work." Photo courtesy of UMSL Black History Project Collection (S0201). 336–705. The State Historical Society of Missouri Photograph Collection.

[think we had] a right to complain? And our answer was: You have black janitors there because it's probably to your economic advantage. And we're gonna picket. Which we did. We maintained a picket out there, and finally—it was early summer—they put one black woman in the doorway, selling ice cream cones. And finally, the economic picket, which was the first economic picket in St. Louis, was successful, and they hired two or three clerks inside the store.

Well, following the success of that, the Colored Clerks' Circle . . . began then to attack all the stores up and down Easton Avenue, and then later, around '32, '33, they branched out. The CCC [was] quite successful in their efforts at opening employment opportunities in the stores in the black ghettos that were operating without any black help, usually family stores.

Although David Grant's oral history doesn't say this, many of those family stores were owned by Jews like my Great-Uncle Jack and almost all of my father's friends and neighbors. The St. Louis Jewish newspapers of the era—there were at least two—occasionally mention conditions for "Negroes" and civil rights, but in the early 1930s the pages were becoming increasingly filled with alarm over the rise of Hitler in Germany and Father Coughlin's rants against Jews.

While the Colored Clerks Circle was picketing with "Don't buy where you can't work" signs in St. Louis, storm troopers across Germany had set up "Don't buy from Jews" pickets blocking access to (the falsely alleged to be Jewish-owned) Woolworth's stores, as well as access to stores actually owned by Jews. The August 18, 1932, *ARGUS* newspaper reported on the Franklin Avenue Woolworth picket, and on the same day, the St. Louis Jewish newspaper *Modern View* reported that a Woolworth in Krefeld, Germany, had been bombed (this was one month after the Nazi Party won a majority in the Reichstag).

In this simmering cauldron, heated by widespread unemployment, racism, and antisemitism, my father put his head down, worked in the family hardware store, and then stepped into his father's junk-dealing business. I don't think he ever had a friend outside of the Ashkenazi Jewish community. At the same time, his sister Rose jumped out of one community and into another.

On January 30, 1933, Adolf Hitler was appointed chancellor of Germany. A few days later, my eighteen-year-old Aunt Gertie in St. Louis, Missouri, began a diary. These two facts have nothing to do with each other. Gertie's diary never mentions anything outside of her close world of friends and family. In my storytelling, though, these two events—one concerning the intimate details of my family's life and the other world shattering for millions of people—form the banks between which flows this section of Aunt Rose's life.

Until Aunt Gertie's diary appeared in a box of old family photos, I had very little firsthand information about what had happened inside my family in the early 1930s. I knew that, in February 1933, my Kinberg family included the siblings Laura, Rose, Tillie, Morrie (my father), Gertie, and Leonard, listed here from oldest to youngest. Aunt Rose was twenty-five and living on her own, estranged but not yet outcast. Aunt Rose's seven-year-old son, Joey, lived with

Rose's mother and siblings. In the wider world, I know that unemployment was high and that the Colored Clerks Circle was picketing for jobs on Franklin Avenue. I know, too, that by the end of February 1933, the Reichstag Fire Decree had eliminated basic civil rights in Germany, inaugurating the Nazi program to segregate Jews and, eventually, to annihilate them.

At this time, my Aunt Gertie was single, dating a few different men, working in an office for a Mr. Burke, and writing her brief diary. Gertie's diary mentions her sister Rose only twice. This first mention reads:

> February 10, 1933. Friday. Woke up this morning with a piece of wood in the sole of my foot. All red and irritated. It pains [me] a lot when I walk on it. I dread to think of baking that cake for Arthur tomorrow for Sunday. What if it should come out badly—I'm sorry I started the whole business. Rose sent Joey, Leonard, and [me] Valentines this morning. I would like to write her, but I am afraid Laura and Mama would object.

Eighteen days later, on the day after the Reichstag fire, Aunt Gertie writes the second—and last—entry with a mention of her sister Rose:

> February 28. I was talking to Mr. Burke today and I learned something awful about Rose. It made me so sick I went home at 2:30. I hadn't eaten any lunch and I got me a Milky Way at some fruit store. It must have been spoilt, 'cause it sure made me feel bad. Went home and took an enema. Helped a little. Washed and tried to curl my hair. Bud came

at 7:30—and as usual I wasn't ready. I wore Laura's black dress, and she fixed my hair real nice. Bud looked darling and as usual handed me a string of compliments.

As reflected in Aunt Gertie's diary, my family members seemed always to be focused inward, on the petty details of family life. The pain of a splinter and the nausea of a bad candy bar merit remembering more than efforts to dismantle segregation or a politically motivated fire in distant Germany. Aunt Rose, though, in her separation from the close-knit family, feels to me drawn into these currents of history.

The mundane details recorded in Aunt Gertie's diary—a splinter in her foot, trepidation about baking a cake, curling her hair and borrowing a black dress for a date—surround a family-rupturing event. Aunt Rose has done "something awful"—perhaps starting to date Mr. Arnwine, perhaps moving to Chicago—which resulted in her permanent separation from her mother, siblings, and son. Meanwhile, all of Jewish life in Germany was being shattered.

In August 1933, the St. Louis Jewish newspaper *Modern View* ran this news article on page 12:

German-Jewish Children to Get "Jim Crow" School Seats

Berlin (WNS)—Beginning with the new school term all Jewish children in the German public schools will have to be seated on special "Jim Crow" benches where their non-Jewish class-mates can easily recognize them, according to a ruling issued to all school officials by the Nazi minister of education, Bernard Rust. Moreover, all school children will

> be obliged to salute their teachers daily with the cry of "Hail Hitler" and regardless of their race will have to participate in the daily singing of the Nazi anti-Semitic songs, many of which call for violence against Jews.

Modern View was an English-language weekly that chronicled the St. Louis Reform Jewish community and was likely one of the papers that was read in my family. I've found in its pages advertisements for my Great-Uncle Jack's Kinberg Hardware store and announcements of engagements, marriages, births, and deaths in my family. Along with pages of social news concerning visits from family, luncheons, vacations, and other various simchas and sorrows, *Modern View* sprinkled in news from Berlin, Palestine, and other places around the world.

The journalist who wrote the brief report from Berlin in 1933 about Jewish schoolchildren drew explicit connections between American anti-Black laws and Nazi antisemitic laws. Although we now know, through the detailed work of James Whitman in *Hitler's American Model*, that the Nazis studied anti-Black laws in the United States while crafting their antisemitic laws, it was not common for this connection to be drawn in American Jewish newspapers in 1933.

The man behind this brief news report, with the byline "Berlin, WNS," named the German anti-Jewish laws "Jim Crow." WNS was the acronym for Worldwide News Service, operated by Joseph Brainin, who merits a biography I hope someone will write someday.

By using the Jim Crow image, Brainin signaled a variety of messages to the Jews in St. Louis who were reading

Modern View. To those who opposed segregation, the article signaled solidarity between Jews and Black people. To those who resisted the civil rights of African Americans, the report might evoke an embellished horror that Jews in Germany could be treated like Black people in the United States. To those Jews, like my father, whose focus was on their own business and family, where racial segregation was the given fabric of life in America, the news from Germany might have irritated some internal tension yet also strengthened the conviction that, in America, Jews must be clearly on the white side of the color line.

I imagine a scene with my father and Aunt Rose at work, she selling dry goods, he selling paint, in separate establishments, both on Franklin Avenue. They each sip their morning coffee and read the small article in the *Modern View* about the Jews in Germany being "Jim Crowed." From outside their shops' doors, they can hear the protesting Colored Clerks Circle chanting, "Don't buy where you can't work." My father's heart is hardened by the tension, while Aunt Rose's heart is opened.

Maybe I'm just looking for a storyteller's device, an imaginary scene in which my characters suddenly pivot, the directions of their lives changing in an instant.

I want to know if there was a moment when their lives diverged, but I can't.

I've often asked friends who have led unconventional lives or lives of activism whether there were particular moments that changed their course. People change their beliefs, their commitments, their values—but how does it happen?

Perhaps my attention to these moments, my sense of their importance, started with the coming-out stories lesbians in the 1970s told each other. As a rite of passage, we asked and were asked: "When did you *know*?" Many stories started with one kiss, one image in a book, or one conversation in which someone said something so awful or so beautiful that you knew you'd never be the same. We had a hunger to know how each of us went from that to this. Every coming-out story changed everything that came before, and would come after, for the teller and the listeners.

How do any lovers meet? My parents met in St. Louis in the late 1930s at the Young Men's Hebrew Association (YMHA). St. Louis Jews of my parents' generation referred to the YMHA as "the Y." Founded in 1880, the St. Louis Y recreation center was heartily used by Jewish immigrants for drama, sports clubs, and socializing. Well into his fifties, my father still sang songs from the *Pirates of Penzance* show that had been performed at the Y when he was in his teens, and he still played handball with the friends he made there. St. Louis Jews will always ask a new acquaintance what high school they attended—high school is a defining signifier. For my father, who went to work at fourteen, when his father died, the Y was his high school.

I met my wife, Patti, forty years ago through a mutual friend in the lesbian community. The friend was one of my housemates, and Patti was in a therapy group with her. We first crossed paths at a Sweet Honey in the Rock concert sponsored by the University of Missouri Women's Center, but I only saw her out of the corner of my eye. Our first introduction was in my kitchen, over a casual dinner.

For my Aunt Rose and Mr. Arnwine, commonplace social meetings would not have been common. Segregation and racism severely limited opportunities for casual acquaintance across racial divides at work, with mutual friends, at a coffee shop or bar, or walking down the street.

When Rose was eight years old, St. Louis had passed legislation to segregate residential neighborhoods, and in the St. Louis of the 1930s, interracial marriages were socially unacceptable, dangerous, and illegal. I try to imagine the commonplace moments when a twenty-something Jewish woman from an Eastern European immigrant family and a thirty-something Black man from Oklahoma could make each other's acquaintance and I'm led into histories of St. Louis that include uncommon interracial events such as musical interests and political organizing. I try to imagine that meeting then leading them into a twenty-year relationship. There must have been elements of their characters, beliefs, and commitments—combined with circumstances—that created an opportunity that Aunt Rose and Mr. Arnwine turned into something lasting.

What were they looking for when they found each other? Was their meeting happenstance or part of a deliberate effort to organize across racial barriers? I can imagine both scenarios: a chance meeting and a result of purposeful organizing.

In telling my aunt's story, I want to conjure up the true Rose; yet at the same time, I long to use her unknowable story to help explore and understand the cloudy and mysterious relationships within my family. I want to understand the life my Aunt Rose led within a Black community beginning in the politically turbulent 1930s, to help me understand my seemingly intrinsic motivations to act for racial and economic justice. Even though I can't confirm my intuitions, I want Aunt Rose's choices to help me understand the roots of my father's virulent racism and anticommunism.

According to political historians, the Communist Party (CP) and associated groups formed the only movement during the 1930s to address racism deliberately through interracial organizing. The policy of the CP in the 1930s was to build the protest movements from the grass roots, from the neighborhoods.

Of all the scenarios I can imagine for Aunt Rose and Mr. Arnwine's first meeting, I want to place them in the crowd on July 11, 1932, at one of the first St. Louis Unemployment Council protests outside St. Louis City Hall. In the depths of the Great Depression, thousands of people listened to three hours of speeches railing against the inadequate administration of relief funds. In newspaper reports on this protest and many others, the Unemployment Council is described as a "communist" organization, or it is said that the protests were organized by "the reds." When I see pictures in the *St. Louis Post-Dispatch* from these protests, I search the crowd of many Black and white faces for Aunt Rose and Mr. Arnwine.

In 1932, Aunt Rose lived on the same block at a separate address from the rest of the family. About a block away, Fannie Feigenbaum, a grassroots leader in the emerging St. Louis Unemployment Council, lived with her family. Aunt Rose and Fannie were the same age, with similar families, living in the same ghetto of Jewish immigrants.

Members of the American Workers Union, a local organization of unemployed individuals, gather outside of St. Louis City Hall on May 12, 1936. The incident that inspired the march was the removal of about fourteen thousand people from the relief rolls on the grounds that they were employable. Photo from the files of the St. Louis Post-Dispatch, *permission from Polaris Images.*

In a 1991 interview with Rosemary Feurer for her book *Radical Unionism in the Midwest, 1900–1950*, Fannie Feigenbaum Goldberg reported how the 1932 protest came about:

> There was no major leader in St. Louis[;] we were just a group of people who believed the same thing. It was small. The first big demonstration, the papers came out with a big headline [announcing] that come Monday the relief would be cut off, whatever little relief there was would be cut off. The Unemployment Councils were just beginning to function. They called a meeting at City Hall. To

> our own surprise, all of St. Louis turned out. So we had a group elected right there, to talk to the Mayor. . . . I mean you can't just cut off relief [for] people who have nothing! Well, the committee couldn't get in. It took about an hour, and the police came and fired tear gas to disperse the crowd. It looked awful because everyone was running away. But it was such a tremendous and big thing that it kind of surprised us. Instead of being intimidated by the attitude, we decided we had to start working.

Newspapers reported that the reds had "stormed city hall."

Feigenbaum Goldberg described the buildup to these demonstrations from her own grassroots perspective, but the organizational backgrounds to these protests reveal intriguing connections between St. Louis and Muskogee, Oklahoma, Zebedee Arnwine's hometown, through the Workers Alliance of America (WAA).

WAA was a training ground for many leaders in local unemployment councils, including the organizers of protests of the unemployed in St. Louis. WAA also organized unemployed Black and white farmers in Muskogee. What's more, I found that in the late 1930s, Edward O. (Aunt Rose's first husband and the father of her son) had remarried and settled in Muskogee with his new wife, opening a dry goods store where he sold dresses sewn in St. Louis. Mr. Arnwine's mother, Catherine; his ex-wife, Tamah; and his daughter with Tamah, Rebecca, all lived near each other in Muskogee. Edward's family lived in a building next to the building where the Black neighborhood began. Catherine Arnwine lived two blocks away and just across the street.

WAA meeting. Muskogee, Oklahoma, 1939. Russell Lee, photographer. Library of Congress, Prints and Photographs Division, FSA/OWI Collection, LC-USF34-033833-D.

I imagine that in a small town in the 1930s, neighbors knew, or least recognized, each other.

There are so many touchpoints of location in my Aunt Rose's life after leaving the Kinbergs. I imagine Aunt Rose and Mr. Arnwine meeting at a protest, organizing for WAA, somehow running into each other in Muskogee. I can't know, yet I can't let it go. Somehow, they met, and sometime between 1933 and 1940, they moved to Chicago.

4

CHICAGO, 1940–1943

No one in 1940 could have foreseen the genocidal violence of the Holocaust or the dropping of nuclear bombs, but warnings were in the air. Looking back from the present day, I see the winds of racial genocides, circulating up high, along with people's hope for lives of abundance.

When President Franklin D. Roosevelt signed into law the Selective Training and Service Act on September 16, 1940, requiring *all men* between the ages of twenty-one and forty-five to register for the draft, every family in the United States had to pause to imagine conscription into war, bringing what was happening in Europe closer to home. Millions of Ashkenazi Jewish families had come to the United States to avoid conscription into armies that did not recognize their humanity, yet now they were being conscripted to fight anti-Jewish fascists. Americans of African descent were still segregated into separate units but were needed for the war effort, raising the hopes of opportunity and change.

I've filled my head with newspaper articles, literature, and photographs produced in those years, and I've read histories and biographies written more recently. Though the turmoil around Aunt Rose and Mr. Arnwine is nearly as present for me as today's headline news, I can't see the world through their eyes—only my own.

I search for photographs to bring me closer to their lives. Two photos from 1941 captivate me. Each is tangentially related to Aunt Rose, and both are so unabashedly optimistic that they make me long to be in the photographer's shoes. My heart races, though, with the knowledge of the trauma and grief on either side of the time frame of these images.

The first photo is a private snapshot of my mother holding my sister, Sheila, who was born in August 1940. My parents had married in September 1939. That they married the month Hitler invaded Poland was never mentioned while I was growing up in St. Louis. As I think about that fact, the coincidence of time indelibly links my family's life into the context of history.

In the 1941 photo, my mother and Sheila are on a back balcony in St. Louis. My mother is waving to someone, and my sister, wearing new baby walking shoes, is looking at the photographer. I love this photo because it captures my mother's confident and resilient nature. Three years before my sister's birth, in 1937, my mother's brother took his own life after being unable to attend medical school because of a quota on Jews at Washington University.

Around the same time, my father lost his sister Rose because his family ostracized her over her marriage to an African American man. I am still trying to unravel my father's feelings about the loss of his sister. As for my mother, I know that her sadness over her brother's suicide never left her.

The other photo is iconic, taken by Russell Lee on assignment for the Farm Security Administration on Easter in 1941, as documentation of the last years of the Great

My mother and my sister Sheila, visiting with my grandmother's brother Max Schwartz, 1941. Personal photo of the author.

Depression. I have viewed this among hundreds of Lee's photographs of Chicago's South Side. Five Chicago boys on the cusp of becoming young men and looking ready to take on anything sent their way sit on a fine car. In researching this photograph, I read that Black families around the country have framed copies of it on their living room walls. It speaks of hope, promise, success.

Aunt Rose and Mr. Arnwine, my mother, these boys—none of them could have known in 1941 what was to come in just a few years: the annihilation of millions of Jews in Europe and the lynching of returning Black soldiers in the United States. In 1941, the year of these very photos, Jews in Poland and Ukraine were being rounded up for mass murder. Jewish men and women in the United States signing up to fight fascism were placed in units with other white Americans who'd never seen a Jew before. I grew up with stories of Christian soldiers feeling the foreheads of Jewish men for the horns they'd been taught grew there.

"Negro boys on Easter morning." South Side, Chicago, Illinois, 1941. Russell Lee, photographer. Library of Congress, Prints and Photographs Division, FSA/ OWI Collection, LC-USF34-038825-D.

While the minutia of Aunt Rose and Mr. Arnwine's lives in Chicago in the early years of World War II remain opaque, the rising pressures on a Black and Jewish interracial couple are palpable.

After the bombing of Pearl Harbor on December 7, 1941, the draft expanded. However, African American men were still limited to segregated units, and most were given the lowest and dirtiest work. In February of 1942, the *Pittsburgh Courier*, a leading Black newspaper, launched the Double V Campaign, for victory against European fascism and victory against Jim Crow racism at home. The campaign was ignited by James Thompson, a twenty-six-year-old Black cafeteria worker in a Cessna aircraft carrier plant in Wichita, Kansas. Cessna did not allow Black workers on the manufacturing floor. Within a few months of the *Courier*'s publication of a letter by Thompson, hundreds of thousands of African Americans had raised the double V banner.

In Black Belt Chicago, despite the pressures of racism, hopefulness still reigned in 1941. Like millions of other African Americans, Mr. Arnwine had left the Jim Crow South and come north to start a new life. I am so grateful to Isabel Wilkerson for chronicling this huge population shift in *The Warmth of Other Suns: The Epic Story of America's Great Migration.* By following the stories of several families (one of them her own forebears) who began in Florida, Mississippi, and Louisiana, and wound up in New York, Chicago, and Los Angeles, Wilkerson beautifully structures her wide-horizoned epic around intimate, personal stories.

Wilkerson tells the story of Ida Mae Brandon Gladney, who moved to Chicago from Mississippi in 1938, around the same time as Aunt Rose and Mr. Arnwine. Gladney had left the Mississippi of Theodore Bilbo, the state's two-term governor and a proud Klansman who'd been elected to the United States Senate in 1935. In 1939, Bilbo introduced into the Senate a bill for the "Voluntary Resettlement of American Negroes in West Africa." After finally losing his reelection campaign in 1947, he published a book titled *Take Your Choice: Separation or Mongrelization.* In Chicago, in 1940, Gladney was able to vote for the first time.

While my father strived to surround his new wife and anticipated children with familiar white Jewish families, his sister Rose moved from St. Louis to Chicago's Black Belt, the near–South Side area of the city that was home to 90 percent of Chicago's Black residents. Aunt Rose moved into a society of complex, roiling currents that were formed when African Americans from all parts of the South pulled up stakes and relocated to the Windy City on Lake Michigan.

In 1910, Chicago's Black population had been 44,000. By 1940, when Aunt Rose and Mr. Arnwine lived there, the Black population of Chicago had grown sevenfold to about 280,000. Yet during those thirty years of growth, the area allowed to Chicago's Black citizens expanded little and became increasingly crowded. White Chicagoans did not only flee to the suburbs as my family had; they used any means necessary to maintain racial segregation in housing. The thrown bricks, bombings, fires, and beatings that accompanied any attempt of Black families to move beyond certain confines were recorded in the *Chicago Defender* and several other Black newspapers.

In order to make room for the people pouring into Chicago, former single-family homes and larger apartments were divided into several "kitchenettes," small apartments with shared bathrooms—just the kind of apartment that three generations of the Younger family in Lorraine Hansberry's groundbreaking play *A Raisin in the Sun* lived in and wanted to escape from.

In Hansberry's play, the white "neighborhood improvement association" offered to pay the working-class Youngers to not move into the house they'd purchased with the elder Mr. Younger's life insurance policy. The playwright refracted traumatic incidents from her own family's lives and wrote the resulting incidents into the play. For example, when Hansberry was eight years old, she was injured by a block of concrete that was thrown through the window of the home her father had purchased in a previously all-white neighborhood just south of Washington Park, less than ten blocks from the kitchenette where Aunt Rose and Mr. Arnwine were living.

As World War II continued, overcrowded Bronzeville in Chicago became its own sort of cauldron in which a person looking for a bit of sun and air might struggle with and against their neighbors. The poet Gwendolyn Brooks captured the atmosphere of dreaming and striving amid the crush in her poem "kitchenette building," published in 1945 in her first book of poetry, *A Street in Bronzeville*: "We are things of dry hours and the involuntary plan / Grayed in, and gray. 'Dream' makes a giddy sound, not strong / Like 'rent,' 'feeding a wife,' 'satisfying a man.'"

Aunt Rose and Mr. Arnwine's kitchenette home on South Michigan Avenue in Bronzeville was located in the midst of a dense and diverse Black neighborhood where the "Chicago Black Renaissance" literary movement was blossoming. Richard Wright and Gwendolyn Brooks, and many other artists, writers, scholars, and activists, including, I imagine, the young Lorraine Hansberry, would meet at the public library on South Michigan, just three blocks north of where my aunt and her husband were living. Black artists and writers organized and presented lectures and other events that informed the coming decades of antiracist social protest. Although I can't see through my aunt's eyes, the cultural legacy of these artists brings me into communion with the lives around her.

Imani Perry, in her biography *Looking for Lorraine: The Radiant and Radical Life of Lorraine Hansberry*, created a bridge between myself and Aunt Rose in its description of Chicago. Born in 1930, Hansberry was a youth during the years Aunt Rose lived in Chicago. She left in 1946 to attend the University of Wisconsin in Madison (where I, too, spent one year, 1972–73). Before completing her degree, Hansberry moved to New York, married a Jewish man, came out to herself as a lesbian, and wrote for leftist publications (and, under a pseudonym, for the lesbian publication *The Ladder*). When she first moved to New York, she wrote for Paul Robeson's *Freedom* periodical, and Robeson, a singer, actor, and activist, became an important mentor for her, introducing her to W. E. B. Du Bois and many others. Hansberry's life as a writer and activist is familiar to me, and I feel connected to her in ways very different from my familial connection to Aunt Rose.

In my telling of this story, the hopes, dreams, constrictions, and violence surrounding Aunt Rose and Lorraine Hansberry become intertwined.

A memory: In the mid-1980s, I would visit Aunt Gertie, Joey's adoptive mother, every week to do odd clerical tasks for her. After her husband died, she lived alone in a small ranch-style home in University City, Missouri. She'd feed me lunch, and we'd talk. In the fall of 1984, Jesse Jackson was running in the Democratic presidential primary, and I wore his button on my lapel. Aunt Gertie commented sardonically, "Times have changed." Her pithy response to my support of Jesse Jackson reflected both the near universal condemnation of Jackson by leaders from her generation of major Jewish organizations and also what she saw as my youthful ability to be inspired by Jackson's "Rainbow Coalition."

Joey, then in his fifties, was living in California, and Aunt Gertie would show me pictures of him as a child along with pictures of her grandchildren. We never once spoke of Aunt Rose, who I now know had died two years prior. Reliving the memory, I feel deep pain and regret thinking that Aunt Gertie may not have even known of her older sister's passing, and I feel this keenly when I consider how I didn't know about her death either, and didn't know to ask.

One afternoon, Aunt Gertie and I had a conversation about Joey and Paul Robeson that has stuck with me. Aunt Gertie had a small record album collection including show tunes, Frank Sinatra albums, a few operas, and one recording that stood out: Paul Robeson's "Ballad for Americans." Written in 1939 and first performed in 1940, "Ballad for Americans" was the anthem of both the Communist Party and the Republican Party presidential nominating conventions that year. "I'm just an Irish, Negro, Jewish, Italian, French and English, Spanish, Russian, Chinese, Polish, Scotch, Hungarian, Swedish, Finnish, Canadian, Greek and Turk and Czech and double Czech American," Robeson sings in his deep voice.

Aunt Gertie explained the album's presence among her other records by saying, "That was Joey's record. He loved it." I wondered: Did he think of his mother, Rose, when he listened to it? Did Robeson's vision of an idealized America help him dream of a reunion—help heal the painful loss of his birth mother? As I pulled that record out of the stack, was Aunt Gertie thinking of Rose, perhaps on the verge of telling me the family stories I most longed—and dreaded—to hear?

The month Paul Robeson first sang "Ballad for Americans" on the radio, November 1940, Lorraine Hansberry's father Carl won his suit in the United States Supreme Court to move south of Washington Park. The *Chicago Defender* announced the victory with a three-inch headline that read, "Hansberry Decision Opens 500 New Homes to Race."

But even with his financial successes in real estate (he was known as "the kitchenette king") and his victory in the Supreme Court, Carl Hansberry came to believe that racism in the United States was too deeply entrenched to change within his lifetime, and by 1946, he was determined to move his family to Mexico. While he was in Mexico finding a house for his family, he died of a brain aneurysm. He was only fifty-one years old, and his daughter Lorraine attributed the stroke to the constant pressures of being a Black man in the United States.

Lorraine Hansberry's first published poem, "Flag from a Kitchenette Window," appeared in the leftist publication *Masses and Mainstream*: "The three-colored banner raised to some / Anonymous freedom, we decide / And on the memorial day hang it / From our window and let it beat the / Steamy jimcrow airs."

Imani Perry points out that this poem is a literary conversation with Gwendolyn Brooks. While the Brooks poem sharply draws the exhausting constriction of life in Bronzeville, attending "carefully to the feelings, senses and space inside the kitchenette apartments," Hansberry's poem "faces outward" and is political, presenting, as Perry writes, "the lives of her father's [kitchenette] residents, people oppressed and exploited, offset against the national lies of liberty and democracy."

As I write this, looking back eighty years, I recognize the gathering, urgent concerns of the 1940s Jewish community and US Black community cascading into separate, unconnected silos. Whether or not individuals had political or religious outlooks that crossed ethnic borders, daily struggles were segregated. The nature of basic lived experiences, from finding and keeping a job and a place to live, to experiencing the dignity of putting on a uniform or waving a flag to represent your country, differed between white Jews and African Americans. For the very few interracial couples, like my Aunt Rose and Mr. Arnwine, troubles could be neither fully shared nor separately siloed.

In my search for Aunt Rose, I heard a story from a cousin in Chicago that Aunt Rose would sometimes travel south from Chicago to St. Louis to see Joey, but she would only watch him from a distance. From her starting point in Chicago, she could have taken the train to the Delmar-Wabash Station, a U. City landmark, which would put our little suburb within reach, with direct service several times a day to and from Chicago. The sleeping cars, which opened at 9:30 p.m., were advertised to passengers with the slogan: "Stay longer at the party—you'll still be on time for your train at the Delmar Station." With such varied travel options, train travel between Chicago and St. Louis was the way to go.

Although the route was convenient, I imagine that the trip from Chicago to St. Louis put Aunt Rose into psychological knots. In St. Louis, among everything familiar, she was part of a family and a community, yet she was also an outlaw.

Did the rhythmic clack of the gliding train accompany her thoughts? I can almost hear her thinking: *Did I make a mistake? Did I make a mistake? Did I make a mistake?*

I conjure Aunt Rose, and she tells me:

When I moved to Chicago, I stewed about Joey all day and night. It tore me up to leave him, but I couldn't have him with me in Chicago. Chicago was six hours and a world away from St. Louis. I was plagued with worry. Did I do the right thing by coming to Chicago?

I had to go back to St. Louis to make sure. There were three Wabash trains each day that went straight to Delmar Station, not far from where Joey attended school. Hy had moved them all into a little apartment on Clemens, right behind the school. Laura's husband was serving overseas, so she and her little twins were living there with Gert, Hy, and Joey. If I got there at the right time, I could see Joey walking to school. I knew he didn't want to see me, but I thought that if I could just catch a glimpse of him, I might stop worrying so much.

Zeb argued with me about going. He was totally against it, sure if I took the train to St. Louis that I'd never come back. I caught what we called the "midnight special." The train had sleeping cars, but I just sat up and dozed a little, arriving in St. Louis in the early morning, when it was still dark.

I walked the few blocks to Clemens, hugging the buildings across the street from the apartment till I could see theirs. Joey came out waving goodbye to the twins, heading off to school. I followed almost a block behind. He never knew.

My son was comfortable in this neighborhood, with friends and family around him all the time. Why was I even thinking that he might want to come to Chicago with me? But me, I'd jumped the color line and would never turn back.

Though she traveled to check on Joey, she returned to Chicago. After moving from St. Louis, Aunt Rose never again lived in a white environment.

Gertie and Hy finalized Joey's adoption in 1939, when the boy was twelve. Their apartment was just a block away from U. City's storied elementary school, Delmar-Harvard, the school Joey might have attended in the sixth grade.

Located in U. City's Loop, Delmar-Harvard was in the heart of a Jewish neighborhood, which, according to longtime *St. Louis Jewish Light* editor Robert Cohn, "was an incredibly secure experience." Cohn continues, "When Jews called U. City 'Jew City,' it was not considered anti-Semitic, it was simply a reflection of perceived demographics."

Delmar-Harvard, which I also attended twenty years later (in the 1960s), was a campus of three large brick buildings, with several playgrounds and an underground tunnel connecting the buildings. It fronted onto Delmar, a major thoroughfare. To the west was the landmark circular University City City Hall, along with other municipal buildings. On the eastern edge of the Delmar-Harvard campus was a white stone retaining wall abutting the playground elevated four feet above the sidewalk. On top of the stone wall was a black, wrought-iron, spoked fence. Something about that edge of the playground always made me anxious, and I never went close to it. The fence collected ominous, dry fallen leaves; the wall seemed to provide cover for lurking strangers. It was an odd feeling because most everything else about the school and the short distance to my home felt familiar and protective. Even at five years old, I walked with other young kids, passing the homes of friends along the few blocks to kindergarten at Delmar-Harvard.

Ethnically focused neighborhoods can be a comfort, but enforced segregation only breeds violence. Racially segregated white neighborhoods exist because of a million little and big, deliberate acts, conditions, laws, practices, regulations, attitudes, and expectations that the white people living there choose to either abet or ignore.

The year my father died (1975), my mother moved to Southern California to a suburban area northwest of Los Angeles. I'd visit her but couldn't wait to get back to my life in St. Louis, where I'd made a home in the Tower Grove neighborhood of the city. My mother's vast and sprawling Los Angeles suburb appeared to me freshly constructed, sun bleached, and deliberately and completely white. My mother's double-wide mobile home park for seniors wasn't completely white, or entirely new, but I was uncomfortable with the contrast between it and my racially mixed St. Louis neighborhood of four-family brick flats. When I visited my mother, I felt angry all the time.

White people in my mother's suburban area had their own insidious California ways of avoiding what, in the 1940s, *Black Metropolis: A Study of Negro Life in a Northern City* called *social equality*. "When white people in Midwest Metropolis [Chicago] express fear that Negroes will demand social equality, they do not mean . . . semi-social acts of courtesy, friendliness, and informal social intercourse. They mean, rather, the prospect of Negroes becoming members of white cliques, churches, and voluntary organizations, or marrying into their families."

Aunt Rose would have been painfully aware of most white people's absolute aversion to social equality. At the same time, while living in Chicago, she would have also experienced how little chasing *social* equality was part of Black life.

Instead, as *Black Metropolis* explains:

> Negroes are generally indifferent to social intermingling with white people, and this indifference is closely related to the existence of a separate, parallel Negro institutional life which makes interracial activities seem unnecessary and almost "unnatural."
>
> Since the 18th century, a separate Negro institutional structure has existed in America. Through the years it has been developing into an intricate web of families, cliques, churches, and voluntary associations, ordered by a system of social classes. This "Negro World" is, historically, the direct result of social rejection by the white society. For Negroes, however, it has long since lost this connotation . . . It is now the familiar milieu in which Negroes live and move from birth to death.

W. E. B. Du Bois used the metaphor of the "veil" to invoke Black life on the side of the color line that white people do not see and cannot experience. Aunt Rose may have recognized her new neighbors' *heymish* feeling of being part of a separate institutional and social structure, so similar to the Jewish family and community she'd left.

Yet, traveling back and forth from Chicago to St. Louis, Aunt Rose would have confronted a heart-stopping difference between the Jewish and Black communities' separateness. Mr. Arnwine's presence as a social equal was absolutely and actively rejected by Rose's family and community, while Aunt Rose's presence as the rare white woman in the Black

Belt—though it might have been occasionally remarked upon—was inconsequential among the community's other joys, sorrows, and challenges.

Black Metropolis devotes one chapter to the estimated four hundred interracial couples that lived in Chicago's Black Belt in the late 1930s. For the book, over 147 extensive interviews were conducted with these couples by white sociologist Robert E. T. Roberts, and the book included this quite intriguing passage from an interview with a white woman: "Some of my sisters and some of my brothers disapproved, but they still wrote and visited me. My other relatives don't approve at all. I have a brother in St. Louis who is very good to me. However, he doesn't approve of my marriage and is ashamed for people to know that his sister is married to a colored man."

The page in my copy of *Black Metropolis* that contains this quote is worn thin. I've parsed every word looking for the definitive clue that this interviewee is Aunt Rose. African American scholar Dorothy E. Roberts (Robert E. T. Roberts's daughter) has the archive of all her father's interviews with interracial couples, and she is working on a book based on the interviews from the period in which Aunt Rose and Mr. Arnwine lived in Chicago.

Aunt Rose and Mr. Arnwine did not settle in Chicago for very long. Their move there in the late 1930s was in the heart of the Great Migration, but the Great Migration's transition from rural South to urban North does not describe their journey's uncommon end.

5

THE MOVE TO MICHIGAN

Finding the *Makom*, the *Mistor*, and the *Miklat*

By 1942, Mr. Arnwine already had a Michigan address on Paw Paw Avenue in Benton Harbor, directly across Lake Michigan from Chicago. He used his Paw Paw Avenue address when he and two other men from Chicago bought twenty-five acres on a lake in Vandalia, Michigan. The three wives were added to the deeds several years later, when they divided the property. My xeroxed deed of sale says they paid $5,000 for the property, which was equivalent to over $90,000 in 2024. I've often wondered whether they'd come into some money somehow or taken out a mortgage. The six of them formed a collective, enabling the purchase of what must have been a quiet, airy dream in comparison to the human crush of Chicago. Little Paradise Lake was about an hour's drive southeast of Benton Harbor, almost to the Indiana border. And so began Aunt Rose's sojourn in the waters of Michiana.

Southwest Michigan was well known within both the Black and Jewish communities for hosting pockets of opportunity and refuge.

It is not hard for me to imagine that Aunt Rose and Mr. Arnwine wanted out of Chicago. As World War II continued, Chicago's South Side, already densely populated, became suffocatingly overcrowded. There were plenty of jobs, but for working-class African American men, employment outside of the Black Belt started at the bottom—in the furnace room or equivalent—and discrimination kept Black workers from advancing. Before the Civil Rights Act of 1964, employers could legally segregate their employees. If they wished, employers could relegate Black women and men to the least secure, lowest-paid jobs. Black professionals in Chicago—doctors, lawyers, politicians, and business owners—were accumulating wealth but still facing considerable confines. Travel and leisure activities such as sports and entertainment at clubs, theaters, and restaurants were limited by racism and segregation.

At the same time, opportunities were opening across Lake Michigan in a region that, while predominantly segregated, also had enclaves of determined antiracist integrationists, farms owned by Black families, resorts for African Americans, other resorts that catered to Jews, and new manufacturing plants that hired all races. Benton Harbor's war boom went beyond Whirlpool, Superior Steel, and Remington Rand, with a growing entertainment economy at its beach resorts and hotels.

Abolitionism and antiracism have long histories in Southwest Michigan. In her 2007 book *A Stronger Kinship: One Town's Extraordinary Story of Hope and Faith* about the growth in the 1800s of the small town of Covert, Michigan, just a few miles north of Benton Harbor, Anna-Lisa Cox tells the story of a community committed to freedom and racial equity. Some of the founders of Covert were Black Civil War veterans from Vandalia, Michigan, who had walked the forty miles to Covert to stake a new claim. Many of the early white pioneers came to Covert as members of a radical, abolitionist, Congregational church influenced by William Lloyd Garrison and Frederick Douglass. *A Stronger Kinship* tells the rare stories of white men loaning Black men needed money to start businesses, all very conscious that "race should not define a man's dreams or hamper his potential." These business transactions were taken with full knowledge that "it was not unheard of in [the] nineteenth-century Midwest for successful Black businessmen to be shot as they stood in their own front yard or to be run out of town for competing with white businesses."

The town's name, Covert, maps onto a new continent the landscape of biblical literature. Cox connects the naming of the small village of Covert in 1876 with the Hebrew word *mistor*, which is often translated as a "covert" and sometimes as a "hidden refuge." Cox writes, "The word [*covert*] connotes concealment and shelter. This community was a symbol of all that white supremacists were arguing was impossible and overtly abhorred. . . . These settlers of Covert were people of great faith [who] were almost certainly aware of this passage from the book of Isaiah: 'There shall be a tabernacle for a shadow in the daytime from the heat, and for a place of refuge, and for a covert from storm and from rain' (4:6)." The connotations of the word *covert* continue further on in Isaiah, which speaks of a "hiding place from the wind, and a covert from the tempest; as rivers of water in a dry place, as the shadow of a great rock in a weary land" (32:2). The Black and white Quaker settlers of the area knew their Bible.

African Americans built other places of refuge in the same Michigan region where Covert was located. Two hours' drive northeast of Covert is the legendary Black lakeside resort town of Idlewild. When W. E. B. Du Bois visited Idlewild in 1920, he was inspired to buy a plot there and wrote in his magazine *The Crisis*, "For sheer physical beauty—for sheen of water and golden air, for nobleness of tree and flower of shrub, for shining river and song of bird, and the low moving whisper of sun, moon, and star, it is the beautifulest stretch I have seen . . . and then to add to that fellowship . . . all sons and grandchildren of Ethiopia, all with the wide leisure of rest and play—can you imagine a more marvelous thing than Idlewild?"

Idlewild was a gathering place for elite African American society, but I imagine all African Americans had heard of it, its reputation something like "Beverly Hills" when I was growing up, a place name that can stand in for the rich and famous. Idlewild was a *miklat*, a place of refuge, but there were other places, more out of the way, quieter places, sheltered by the surrounding woods and farms. Vandalia, Michigan, was such a *mistor*.

In 1940, daily ferries traveled over Lake Michigan from Chicago to Benton Harbor, carrying vacationers, tourists, and seasonal workers. Benton Harbor boasted the "world's largest open-air fruit market," and surrounding farms supplied produce direct from farmers to individuals, restaurants, and brokers in the whole region, including Chicago.

On a frigid Chicago day, perhaps Aunt Rose or Mr. Arnwine saw the ad in the February 17, 1940, issue of the *Chicago Defender*, put there by Dr. C. A. Mott of South Bend, Indiana, for forty acres of land near Paradise Lake, Michigan. It wasn't the lake of Idlewild but a different small lake just north of Indiana, in Cass County.

Dr. Cassel A. Mott was a respected family doctor who, like many African Americans in South Bend, had ties to Cass County, Michigan, and to Chicago. Perhaps Aunt Rose made some inquiries, took the ferry over to Michigan, brainstormed how to come up with the money. Maybe Aunt Rose and Mr. Arnwine talked up the possibilities with some friends: Across the street from their kitchenette, on the other side of South Michigan Avenue, lived Leon and Ivie, and a few blocks away, Lionel and Jewel. All of them would likely have heard of Idlewild, where the wealthiest and most influential of their neighbors vacationed.

In the 1940s, the official highway map issued by the Cass County Road Commission was titled "Cass County: The playground of Southwestern Michigan." The map lists popular lakeside fishing spots and boating resorts. Out of the dozens of named locations, Paradise Lake near Vandalia is notably the only place listed as "a tourist resort lake devoted to colored people."

Three Black Chicago doctors, including the nationally known, trailblazing dermatologist Dr. Theodore K. Lawless, invested in land on Paradise Lake and built a small hotel. Historians of the region have taken oral histories from Vandalia locals who report that Dr. Lawless and the others were hoping to replicate the success of Idlewild, though perhaps on a smaller scale. Within three years of Dr. Mott's ad in the *Chicago Defender*, Aunt Rose and Mr. Arnwine, Leon and Ivie, and Lionel and Jewel together bought land on that same lake in Michigan.

Imagining this move, from Chicago to Paradise Lake in Vandalia via Benton Harbor, brings me so close to Aunt Rose that I can almost inhabit her. I had moved from St. Louis to the Ozarks and also to rural Oregon. In the countryside, the soothing quiet and oxygen-filled air, the morning sun glinting off the dew, seemed to bring my soul to the surface of my skin. Aunt Rose, did you feel this, too?

When I discovered that the aunt whom I'd never met lived most of her life in what was then the most racially mixed rural county in the entire Midwest, I was awestruck. She had found what I had been looking for.

Paradise Lake is situated between the town of Vandalia and the farming communities of Calvin and Porter Townships. On old maps, the lake on which Vandalia sits was labeled "Mud Lake." Along the way, it was renamed Paradise Lake. This name, too, has traditional Jewish connotations.

The English word *paradise* is similar to words meaning "enclosed garden," "park," or "orchard" in Old French, Latin, Greek, Persian, Arabic, Hebrew, and Sanskrit. The Hebrew word *pardes* is often used in biblical texts to denote a cultivated place of beauty and abundance and a place of divine blessing. In addition, in the Jewish cultural tradition of using word play during study, the acronym PRDS or PaRDes is a mnemonic device to help remember four approaches to reading the text of Torah: *P'shat* means "surface" or "literal"; *remez* means "hints," "hidden," "allegoric," or "symbolic"; *derash* means "seeking" similar occurrences of and connections between words and events; and *sod* means "secret" or "mystical."

Just as Jewish tradition teaches many approaches to reading the Torah, there are also many—some say seventy-two—names for God. These names are often associated with particular eras of human history. While never pronouncing the four Hebrew letters *yud*, *hey*, *vav*, *hey* as they are written in text, Jews today often use *HaShem* (the Name) because God has no name, and *HaMakom* (the Place) because God has no place.

Yet the stories in the Torah are all about the Israelites finding a place, a *makom*, to call home. The Hebrew word *makom* has many English translations: "city," "land," "region," "locality," "spot," "space," "room," "quarter," "direction." The land the Israelites seek while wandering in the desert is literal and symbolic, a corporeal place that is connected to other places on earth and that also can reveal spiritual and mystical wisdom. In Genesis 28:10–22, Jacob has a dream of encountering God, and he gives a name to the place, the *makom*.

The Book of Job, though, speaks not of land but of *makom bina* as the place of understanding and *makom chochma* as the place of wisdom. Jacob names the place where he encounters God Bethel (House of God). The text says that the place had a name before Jacob named it. Hittites who lived there called it Luz, which means "almond tree." After waking from his dream of encountering God, Jacob says, "God is in this place, and I, I did not know it!"

I think about these layered meanings when I visit the place, Paradise Lake, where Aunt Rose chose to live. As I turn south off Interstate 94 onto the narrow roads leading to her rural community, I open the car windows to breathe in the country air. I slow down and experience a simultaneous feeling of descending and ascending—lowering into a hidden covert and refuge, yet also climbing an elevation, a path up a mountain built of the actions of humans over many generations. The place where Aunt Rose settled has played a quiet yet outsize role in North American history.

The 185 acres of Paradise Lake are near the center of a large watershed that gathers rainfall and underground water into the St. Joseph River, named by French missionaries in the late 1600s. The river winds through hundreds of miles of prairie, hillocks, and wetlands. The St. Joseph River empties into the massive Lake Michigan, and it is the lake's third-largest tributary of fresh water. The rounded rhombus-shaped land area of the St. Joseph River Basin watershed was the homeland for thousands of years of Potawatomi peoples, who traveled by canoe through the rivers and lakes of the watershed's fertile, abundant wetlands. Thousands of years.

The headwater of the St. Joseph River is eighty miles directly east of Paradise Lake, in Baw Beese Lake near Hillsdale, Michigan. The Potawatomi leader Baw Beese, for whom the headwater lake is named, lived during the European invasion and endured the forced removal of his people to Kansas and Oklahoma in the 1840s, which continued into the 1850s.

The watershed, with streams above- and underground, draws together life from parts of fifteen administrative counties, including the townships of South Bend, Goshen, and Elkhart in Indiana, and Niles, Cassopolis, Dowagiac, Calvin, Vandalia, and Three Rivers in Michigan. The places where Aunt Rose spent her days are all connected through streams, rivers, and lakes. As the St. Joseph River reaches Lake Michigan, it forms a watery boundary between the townships of Benton Harbor and St. Joseph, twin cities where the most bitter legacies of white racism shape the human landscape. Residents of St. Joseph, which is today 85 percent white, have three times the family income and homes valued at more than three times those of the residents of Benton Harbor, which is 85 percent Black and has a reputation for a damningly high crime rate. The striving interwar Jewish community in Benton Harbor, with small shops and growing families, is no longer there.

As the waters of Baw Beese Lake flow and mingle with all the waters of the St. Joseph River watershed, human actions upstream affect life downstream, with dreams and good intentions, disappointments and waste, carried from one creek to another.

Hillsdale College, located on the shore of Baw Beese Lake, was founded in 1844 by abolitionist Free Will Baptists. From the beginning, it has been nondenominational, and has admitted "all persons irrespective of nation, color or sex," becoming one of the only racially integrated colleges at that time, as well as the second college in the nation to grant four-year liberal arts degrees to women. Before the Civil War, it was actively antislavery and was visited by Frederick Douglass, and its leadership helped to found the Republican Party, which nominated Abraham Lincoln for the US presidency.

A little over one hundred years after its founding, Hillsdale College's values were tested and revealed on the national stage. Its undefeated 1955–56 football team was invited to the Tangerine Bowl in Florida, an opportunity to win a national championship. But the Hillsdale College team declined the invitation to play the championship game when they learned that their four Black players would not be allowed on the field. (It wasn't until the late 1960s that white and Black college football players could compete against each other.)

The football coach Frank "Muddy" Waters had spent months lobbying to allow his team to compete. Not only was college football segregated but the city of Orlando, Florida, where the game would be played, also did not allow integrated bleachers. Little Hillsdale College knew having an integrated team challenged the whole Jim Crow system. Hillsdale hails the team's decision to stand against discrimination as a "better kind of glory."

However, just as a national movement against discrimination was gathering steam in the early 1960s, and just as the manufacturing boom in Benton Harbor was crashing, leaving behind environmental disasters and masses of unemployed people, Hillsdale College separated itself from the movement that confronted the disproportionate consequences suffered by African Americans.

Hillsdale College describes its subsequent history this way: After Civil Rights legislation in the 1960s, their moral values led them to reject all money coming from the federal government. Their "color-blind" policies meant that they would not report the racial makeup of their student body anymore and therefore would not participate in the national efforts to secure civil rights. They raised a huge private endowment, allowing them to reject even federally funded grants or loans to individual students. Over the ensuing decades, Hillsdale College's reputation grew as one of the nation's most conservative institutions.

By 2016, Hillsdale College had transformed into a gushing fount of support for Donald Trump and particularly for Federalist Society–style judicial activism, which insists that the US Constitution's meaning be frozen in time, interpreted according to the intent of its long-dead authors—many of whom were slaveholders, and all of whom were white men. Hillsdale's current leadership was overjoyed by Trump's appointment of 226 judges who adhere to this originalist judicial philosophy. And although the college rejects all financial connections to the federal government, in 2015 the college opened a second campus in Washington, DC, where its Center for Constitutional Studies and Citizenship and its Graduate School of Government helped create the so-called 1776 Curriculum. This curriculum teaches the college's beliefs about American history and counters the antiracist 1619 Project Curriculum, which centers the consequences of slavery and the contributions of Black Americans in the narrative of US history.

During the decades of Hillsdale's transformation, crosscurrents from the Civil Rights Movement and the concomitant white backlash washed through the entire human landscape of the St. Joseph River watershed, dropping silt even in the covert created by the farmers of Calvin Township, descendants of enslaved individuals, freeborn Black people, Native Americans, and antislavery Quakers.

Calvin Township and the little village of Vandalia were a haven—for a while, for some—yet the racism that created the need for such refuge unceasingly lurked and seeped into the lives of the people living there.

One of those descendants is my friend Marshall H. Sanders Jr., whose parents and my Aunt Rose are buried near each other in the Calvin Community Chapel Cemetery. In 1935, Marshall's parents moved from Vandalia to Detroit, where Marshall was born in 1940. At the beginning of each summer break throughout his school years, he and his brother would pack up their bicycles and go stay with their grandparents in Vandalia until Labor Day. Later, in 1958, he began attending Hillsdale College, where he spent four years in small-town Michigan, near the headwaters of the St. Joseph's River Basin. His commitment to the region and its people goes deep.

Marshall is a story keeper for Vandalia, Paradise Lake, and the community. He treasures his mother's carefully kept scrapbooks and passes on stories of the place and its people. Marshall visits the cemeteries of Cass County every year, and it is through a cemetery that I met him.

Aunt Rose's death certificate listed Calvin Community Chapel Cemetery as the place she wanted to be buried. With very little trouble, I found pictures online of this cemetery in rural Cass County, Michigan. Marshall H. Sanders Jr. had photographed many of the gravestones in the cemetery and uploaded them, in 2006, to the USGenWeb Tombstone Photo Project. However, there was no Rose Arnwine listed among several hundred names.

Calvin Community Chapel Cemetery, where Aunt Rose is buried. Photo by Marshall H. Sanders Jr. used with permission.

"Mr. Sanders, I see you've photographed some graves in Cass County, Michigan," I wrote in an email to the address that accompanied the cemetery photos. "I am looking for the resting place of an aunt of mine, my father's sister. Do you think she has a place in Calvin Community Chapel Cemetery?" I attached Aunt Rose's death certificate.

So began my first lesson in anxiously awaiting answers from people who found Rose Kinberg Arnwine's life (and death) less urgent than I. Waiting—and carrying on with my life—would become my normal state of being. While I wondered whether my email had even reached Marshall, I embarked on a cross-country family road trip to drop off my older daughter at college in Oregon.

On August 15, 2016, almost two weeks after I'd sent my missive into the ether, Marshall finally responded. I was somewhere in the high country outside of Zion National Park in Utah, rounding a mountain pass when I heard my phone ding.

From the first, Marshall was gracious and involved; he wanted to help me find what I was looking for. Marshall, I learned, was not only familiar with the cemetery listed on Aunt Rose's death certificate but also had family members—his parents—buried there. To this day, he visits the cemetery often. In this first correspondence, he also wrote, "While it is not impossible she is buried at Community, this cemetery is predominately African American." *Perhaps she is down the road at the white cemetery*, he implied.

My first interaction with Marshall left me with the clue that, in death at least, race mattered in Vandalia: The cemeteries were presumed to be segregated.

Marshall's roots in Cass County go back to 1849, when a white Virginia farmer, Sampson Sanders, died and in his will manumitted approximately fifty-one people whom he had owned. In her book *Cabell County's Empire for Freedom: The Manumission of Sampson Sander's Slaves*, Carrie Eldridge details "one of the most unusual events . . . in all of early Virginia in a period when very few slave masters freed even one slave."

Free people of African descent could not live in Virginia. The manumission was provisioned on the group of families and coworkers, including seven babies under the age of two, being relocated to Indiana or one of the other free states. The oldest individuals of the group were Zebedee Sanders and his wife, Ada, both eighty-seven years old. This Zebedee, born in 1763, is Marshall's fourth great-grandfather.

The will also designated money, provisions, farm equipment, and three white lawyers to travel with the families over river raft, train, and wagon to find their new homes. The Missouri Compromise and Fugitive Slave Act of 1850, which required all citizens to assist in the capture of runaway slaves, had not yet become law but was being drafted for debate in Congress. In addition to deterring slave catchers, the white lawyers were charged with making sure the property each family bought was of good value for farming.

Manumission, the legal pathway for slave owners to release people from bondage, is viewed by many contemporary historians as a leg that supported the institution of slavery, its concept built on the immoral logic of white supremacy and chattel slavery in which all agency is reserved for the slave holders.

In early October 1849, the families formerly owned by Sampson Sanders were ready to launch their flotilla on the Guyandotte River. By this time, the "free state" of Indiana had passed very stringent laws severely restricting the lives of free Black people. However, right across the state line, north into Michigan, land was affordable, and there were already fifty or so Black families farming land they owned in the central townships of Cass County. That is where the flotilla headed. By October 12, 1849, the Sanders families were already claiming deeds in Cass County.

The Black farming community the Sanders families joined had settled in Michigan territory in the early 1830s (Michigan didn't become a state until 1837). They had come from Illinois, North Carolina, Virginia, Ohio, Indiana, Kentucky, and Tennessee. People escaping slavery and free Black families found relatively inexpensive frontier land here, and a local white population influenced by Quakers, who were actively opposed to slavery. In her thesis "Surviving Freedom: African American Farm Households in Cass County, Michigan 1832–1880," Marcia Renee Sawyer's loving and respectful scholarship delves into race relations and the strategies Black frontier farm families used that formed the foundation of Cass County's unique culture.

African Americans came to Cass County "to escape a proscriptive and racist environment that prevented them from voting, educating their children, and moving freely within their native state to ply a trade, seek employment, or merely to visit a friend," Sawyer explains. White Quakers came to the area because it was on the known route of the Underground Railroad from Indiana and up to Canada. They came to oppose slavery.

Sawyer writes that at this early time, Black families tended to try to keep under the radar. They came with useful frontier skills learned earlier in life and went to work to build homesteads for their families. A stagecoach on the Detroit–Chicago line occasionally stopped nearby.

Cass County entered the history books when, in 1847, a group of about forty Kentucky slaveholders raided Michigan looking for their "property," instigating what came to be called the Kentucky Raid, an important turning point in the buildup to the Civil War. The slave catchers captured nine people across several farms in Cass County. Reputedly, three hundred Cass County residents, including Quakers, free Black people, and other abolitionists, confronted the Kentuckians in Vandalia. According to the Underground Railroad Society of Cass County, the confrontation "ensued at O'Dells Mill in Vandalia and the Kentuckians brandished weapons. The Quakers present were credited with calming the situation before it escalated into further violence. Because they were outnumbered, and because they believed the law was clearly on their side in light of the

Fugitive Slave Act of 1793, the Kentuckians agreed to go to Cassopolis and stand trial."

The commissioner who heard the case was an abolitionist and a conductor on the Underground Railroad who decided against the Kentuckians. "Colored men are not property in Michigan," he reportedly said, and he allowed the freed people to travel up to Canada and sent the slave catchers back to Kentucky.

The backlash was severe and led to the passing of the Fugitive Slave Act of 1850, which was designed to demand the return of fugitive slaves no matter where they were caught. This further inflamed the tensions that led to the Civil War.

The Arnwine and Sanders families both had unusual histories with pre–Civil War manumission. The wills of both Albartis Arnwine in Texas and Sampson Sanders in Virginia required the freed people to move to other states and provided resources for the move. While the Sanders families were staking out their land and planting their first crops in Cass County, the Arnwines in Texas were denied freedom and had their resources stolen.

For the storyteller in me, the correlations between these rare freedom stories draw my attention, creating almost a sense of destiny around Aunt Rose and Zebedee Arnwine's move to Cass County, a place that had a history of providing refuge.

Marshall's mother, Esther (née Wilson) Sanders, was born the same year as Aunt Rose, 1908. She was descended from the earliest Black settlers in the Cass County area and was among a group of people who in 1928 founded a nondenominational congregation and organized the building of the Calvin Community Chapel, which later became known as the Stone Chapel. The membership raised money for the chapel by preparing dinners, giving concerts, and putting on plays. I learned the details of the building's construction, all done by volunteers, from a booklet printed in 1978 for the fiftieth anniversary of the Calvin Community Chapel that Marshall provided to me. The oldest volunteer was eighty-four (born in 1846). Especially poignant to me were the details about the masonry and collection of the stones:

> During construction men of the church used teams of horses with scoops to remove dirt for the basement. . . . Logs were furnished by different members . . . In 1930 stones were hauled to the building site. . . . Ladies of the church and children gathered stones from a pit near Williamsville. . . . Members and friends gathered stones from their fields. Special stones treasured by members of the community were brought to the masons and placed in prominent places in the front of the building. The stone work of the church was completed by November 1, 1930.

To help retire the debt incurred from building the stone chapel, forty-five members pledged to pay one dollar each per month.

When she married Marshall Sanders Sr. in 1935, Esther Wilson already had a teaching degree and a bachelor of arts degree in biological sciences from the University of Michigan. The couple moved to Detroit and raised their sons there, but they brought Marshall Jr. and his brother Maurice back to Vandalia every summer.

My first exchange with Marshall had instilled doubt: Could Aunt Rose have been buried in a Black cemetery?

Calvin Community Chapel during construction in 1931. Photo courtesy of Marshall H. Sanders Jr.

I had to follow up, but I waited until I was back in Michigan from the ten-thousand-mile sojourn out west to drop off my daughter for her freshman year of college. As soon as I got in the door, I contacted the funeral home listed on Aunt Rose's death certificate. The helpful director found Aunt Rose's thin file containing a newspaper clipping of her brief obituary and the plot number of her burial site, indeed in the Calvin Community Chapel Cemetery where Marshall's parents rest. The director then added information that he suspected had been supplied by her friends: "As for family, a note on the record says that she has family someplace, including a son, but that they had disowned her." The obituary had ended with, "There are no known survivors."

Evidently, Aunt Rose had purchased a small section of the cemetery and was buried in an unmarked grave near some friends. The funeral home advised me that the sexton and cemetery caretaker, Bill Vaughn, may have known the location of Aunt Rose's grave and gave me a number for him.

On my first visit to Vandalia, I met Mr. Vaughn at Aunt Rose's unmarked grave. It was Monday, September 5, 2016—Labor Day—when my wife, Patti, my daughter Zevi, and I made the two-hour trek to the other side of Michigan and pulled into the drive of a small cemetery next to a stone church. I recognized the building from Marshall Sanders's photos. The cemetery was sparse, with little hillocks, not more than an acre or two. At the end of the small drive was a pickup truck facing the road. As I got out of our car, a man my age—in his early sixties—stepped out of the truck, and we walked toward each other. Mr. Vaughn was a tall man with a freckled, light-brown face and pinkish cheeks. The first thing he said to me was, "I believe you favor your aunt."

"Oh really?" I said, "You knew her?" My calm voice concealed, I hoped, an erupting surge of emotion.

"I remember meeting her when I was younger. I think I hauled some gravel for her driveway." Mr. Vaughn was the first person I talked to in Vandalia who knew Aunt Rose. And he had dug her grave, literally.

Patti and Zevi stayed in the car while Mr. Vaughn and I walked through a few rows of gravestones to an empty spot in the row closest to the church. Mr. Vaughn told me that this was where Aunt Rose was buried. I wandered around the space, taking note of the names of the nearest marked graves: Sanderses, Wilsons, Mifflins, and a McGee. Perhaps her friends, her adopted family—perhaps clues to her life.

I wondered whether Aunt Rose felt embraced here, among her community, so far from her birth family.

The cemetery where most of our family rests, Chesed Shel Emeth (Kindness and Truth) in University City, Missouri, is very familiar to me. Several dozen of my relatives are buried there, including Aunt Rose's mother and father, her grandfather and grandmother, all three of her brothers, and a sister.

I've walked the narrow paths of Chesed Shel Emeth countless times. I love to stand in the midst of the gravestones and be enclosed in its familiarity. In 1897, my great-grandmother (my father's—and Aunt Rose's—grandmother) was buried in Chesed Shel Emeth when she died ten days after giving birth to my Great-Aunt Mary. It was in the first years of the cemetery, when the Chesed Shel Emeth Society buried Russian Jews who didn't have the money for a plot or a headstone. Chesed Shel Emeth in my mind's eye is a shtetl, a small Jewish village—the home of the poor, and the very poor, all laid up next to the better off. There's a plethora of peddlers, tailors, and junk dealers, like my father, grandfather, and great-grandfather, buried there.

When my mother died a few months after my first visit to Vandalia, I found invoices and paid checks from my father and his brother to the Chesed Shel Emeth Society, beginning in 1951, the year my paternal grandmother died. My father and uncle had paid for several plots on a regular basis through the 1960s.

Every name on a headstone in Chesed Shel Emeth Cemetery echoes with the voices of familiar teachers, neighbors

Chesed Shel Emeth Cemetery in University City, Missouri, where over forty of my relatives are buried. The author's photo.

and schoolmates, grocers and shoe salespeople, teammates, cousins, and friends. Of the seventeen thousand people buried in Chesed Shel Emeth—so many families like mine with generations buried there—I think I am connected, through marriage and proximity, to each and every one. When I walk the rows of the cemetery, I look at each headstone and think, I know you, I know you, I know you.

Two months after my first trip to Vandalia and the Calvin Community Chapel Cemetery, when I first stood near my Aunt Rose's unmarked grave, I drove the same route to the rural southwest Michigan county where she and her husband, Zebedee Arnwine, had made their home.

This time I went alone. In the cold and soggy first week of November 2016, the "Trump for President" signs were posted everywhere, on rusted silos and half-painted barns. Trump country makes me uneasy, and I was unsure of my safety as a Jewish lesbian woman traveling alone. The MAGA signs seemed to broadcast, "Gay Jewish strangers go away."

In the small town of Cassopolis, the county seat, feelings of anxiety and alienation crept into me, tightening my skin as I tried to find the Cass County Historical Library and the Recorder of Deeds Office.

I found the office late in the afternoon, too late to do more than scratch the surface of the information stored there. Within a half hour, though, I laid my hands on the original deed to the twenty-five acres of Paradise Lake waterfront that Mr. Arnwine had bought for $5,000 in 1943. There were two other men on the deed, Lionel Glover and Leon Amico—my Aunt Rose was not named. I left the office with a photocopy of the papers, a satisfying accomplishment. I'd be back to search for more on a later trip.

As I left Cassopolis just after 5 p.m., when the November dusk sets in, I noticed two lonely but appreciated "I'm with her," "Clinton for President" signs. The 2016 election would be over the following week. I might have foreseen then that Trump would take Michigan, but I didn't.

In April of 2017, I made another trip to Vandalia, driving through spring greenery and freshly plowed, rolling fields ready to be planted. I first descended and then rose into an almost familiar landscape.

On this trip, grain silos looked new and shiny, ready to receive the corn that was yet to be planted. The route was comfortable, and even when the GPS lost its signal, I knew where I was headed—south, then west. I knew where to park and how to find my way through the labyrinth of county offices to the Recorder of Deeds Office's small rooms, which housed ledgers filled with each and every Cass County real estate transaction from the 1800s onward.

In these rooms, with growing awe and thankfulness, I found at least a dozen deeds related to Aunt Rose and Mr. Arnwine. Moreover, I found their divorce decree from 1957, and, with real surprise, I found deeds involving Catherine Arnwine, Mr. Arnwine's mother, from as early as 1951, when she assumed the mortgage on thirty-four nearby acres. I realized that Mr. Arnwine and Aunt Rose were married for a full twenty years (from the late 1930s to the late 1950s) before their acrimonious (discerned from the decree) divorce, and that they'd had family close by. His mother was a part of their lives starting in the same year Aunt Rose's mother passed away.

In 1943, when they purchased the land, only the three husbands (Mr. Arnwine, Mr. Amico, and Mr. Glover) were listed on the deed of sale, but when they divided the land into separate parcels six years later, in 1949, each was listed on a deed with his wife. "Zebedee W. Arnwine and Rose Arnwine, husband and wife," were deeded 10.76 acres; "Lionel Glover and Jewel Glover, husband and wife," were deeded 5.38 acres; and "Leon Amico and Ivie Amico, husband and wife," were deeded 5.38 acres. Because I could never find a marriage certificate for Aunt Rose and Mr. Arnwine, seeing the phrase "husband and wife" on the deed was very important. I also found a section of a probate document related to Rose Arnwine's will.

The legal papers were full of information, and confusing. The facts were scrambled and hard to decipher. Ownership of properties seemed to be established over and over, implying that ownership was disputed. I realized I had a full trove of research waiting for me in these ledgers.

In their divorce decree in 1957, Aunt Rose became full owner of the 10.76 acres on Paradise Lake and relinquished any claim to any other property Mr. Arnwine may have owned.

Over the next twenty years, Aunt Rose mortgaged the property, divided it, and sold it, sometimes providing owner financing. When she died in 1982, her will specified the dispensation of each plot to which she and her financial partners still held mortgage.

I also found a document, dated six months after Aunt Rose's death, titled "Order Allowing Final Account and Assigning Residue of the Estate of Rose Lillian Arnwine, Deceased." She assigned her personal property and real estate in the amount of $15,953.84 (a not-insignificant sum, especially in 1982) to Margaret Davis and Ann McGee—new names to investigate, though I remembered a McGee was buried in the plot next to Aunt Rose's in the Calvin Community Chapel Cemetery. The final account was presented to the court by "Cinda Saylor, personal representative."

Still naive about the laws of wills, I thought, at the time, that "personal representative" could mean a personal friend, a person who knew Aunt Rose. I thus determined to track down Cinda Saylor, who, according to the internet, was sixty-eight years old and still living in the area.

As the sun lowered on the horizon, I drove to the address listed on the court document from 1982, thirty-five years prior. After nervously passing by the house three times, I finally pulled into the driveway of a large, rambling, colorfully painted two-story home with a wraparound porch. Two white-haired white people were sitting on the porch. As I stuck my head out of the car window with no plan in mind, I shouted, "I'm looking for Cinda Saylor." The woman replied, "That's me!" as the other person retreated inside.

I tumbled out of the car waving a stack of xeroxed copies, still yelling because I didn't—and still don't—like to approach people I didn't know unless invited, "You're listed on my Aunt Rose's will from 1982 as a personal representative, and . . ."

"I never met her," Cinda snapped, and then she inexplicably softened, "but I worked for a few lawyers back then and did things like that. I think I remember that name. Rose is such a pretty name. . . ."

Cinda walked down to my car and we started to look through the papers, which she said she likely typed up. I explained that I was just looking to find my aunt's personal effects, things like photos, letters—small things that may have been hers. She looked at the names Margaret Davis and Ann McGee, the women to whom Aunt Rose left her things. Cinda told me that she had lived in the area all her life—perhaps in this same house, I thought—but that she didn't recognize these names. As we spoke, she fixated on placing the lawyer she had worked for in 1982, trying to relate it to the date of her own marriage, when she changed jobs and worked for the county, or another lawyer, when she retired. . . .

Finally, Cinda looked up, examined my face, and asked, "Was your aunt white or Black?"

Never quick on my feet, I answered simply: "My aunt was white and her husband was Black." My mind was working overtime with questions I hadn't asked: I wanted to know more about the texture of my aunt and Mr. Arnwine's lives as an interracial couple in rural southwest Michigan—yet my blunt answer to her question shut down Cinda, and I felt I'd blown this opportunity to find out anything more from her.

"Nope. I didn't know her," she concluded, giving me a look that indicated she didn't have anything more to say, so I hopped back into the car and drove away.

On Memorial Day in 2018, two years after I first contacted Marshall about his cemetery photos, he and his wife, Sharon, took me on a tour of the Black cemeteries of Cass County. The oldest, Chain Lake, was founded in 1838 and includes Marshall's great-great-great-great-grandparents.

We'd started to plan this trip in October the year before, but the first snowfall came the very night of our conversation about going together to Vandalia. Snow continued for six months, through April. Driving to rural, hilly Vandalia is unwise in winter, so we'd been waiting for a day just like this one: sunny and breezy with unthreatening clouds. Since Marshall and Sharon were driving from another part of Michigan, we made a plan to meet in Vandalia at 10:30 a.m., across from the fire station on Paradise Lake Road.

A brief rain freshened the air during my two-hour drive. I arrived in Vandalia at the agreed-upon time but couldn't find the fire station even after circling the lake twice. Paradise Lake Road, where the inviting cabins looked ready for summer, hugs the north and east shores of the lake. Brownsville Street, where my Aunt Rose had lived for forty years, runs along the south side of the lake, with homes set back into overgrown fields and down hidden lanes.

After twenty minutes of circling, I found Marshall and Sharon waiting for me at the appointed corner. I apologized for getting lost and delaying their day. They showed me a bag full of bright plastic flowers they planned to leave on graves, and we headed off to the first cemetery on Marshall's list.

The first cemetery on our tour had rolling hills of old stones in family plots and freshly mown grass. The quiet of the cemetery was broken by the whirring of a Weedwhacker wielded by a small figure in the gully near the road. Chain Lake Cemetery, together with the church overlooking Chain Lake, is a Michigan historic site, the second-oldest Black church in Michigan, which was once visited by Booker T. Washington and Sojourner Truth. In 1903 (around the time Aunt Rose's mother, Yetta Schwartz, arrived in the United States from Romania), Washington published a laudatory essay focused on the prosperous, self-sufficient Black community in Vandalia. This essay, "Two Generations Under Freedom," appeared in *The Outlook*, a popular weekly magazine. While visiting the cemetery, I touched the gravestones of the people Washington interviewed for the essay.

Marshall's relatives seemed to be in every corner of the cemetery. I wandered around on my own for a while, giving Marshall and Sharon a little privacy to sort out the flowers and the graves.

From Chain Lake, we went on to the secluded Mount Zion Cemetery. There was no marker for this one—just a break in the trees. Marshall showed me the corner where some of the oldest graves were almost melting into the earth.

After exploring the Mount Zion Cemetery, Sharon and Marshall were already running out of flowers even though we still had one more cemetery to go. Instead of immediately moving on, we paused at Mount Zion for some snacks. In the shade of large oak and maple trees, Sharon and Marshall pulled three chairs out of their trunk. A cooler with cut-up watermelon appeared along with plates, forks, napkins, and several varieties of chips. In great detail, Marshall told some colorful stories of the early settlers of the area, as if he'd seen it all himself. I imagined it was his mother and grandmother talking through him, stories they, in turn, had heard from their grandparents. Marshall was a griot, a maggid, a preserver of history.

I told them I was working on a book about Aunt Rose, about Vandalia.

On to the third stop, at Calvin Community Chapel Cemetery, where Marshall's parents—and my Aunt Rose—were buried.

Marshall and Sharon, and Marshall's brother Maurice, have already bought and installed in this cemetery black granite headstones engraved with their genealogy. On Marhsall's stone is his father's line, from his fourth great-grandfather Zebedee, to Solomon, Levi, Calvin, and Oscar, and then to Marshall Sr., all buried in Cass County. Also engraved was his mother's line, with even deeper roots in Cass County. Visiting these graves, with each person's stories rising from the earth and grass into the air we breathed, was a timeless blessing.

Marshall and Sharon dusted off the freshly mown grass while I wandered up to the unmarked spot the cemetery sexton, Mr. Vaughn, had pointed to on my first trip to Vandalia a year and a half earlier. I had found the spot Aunt Rose chose to be buried, but I hadn't found her. Her resting place, with no designation, seemed to me to be hiding her.

A legal notice published in the *St. Louis Daily Record* on December 31, 1938, declared: ". . . appearing to the satisfaction of the Court from the verified petition for the adoption this day filed herein, that Rose, mother of Joseph Irwin, a minor, who Hyman Polinsky and Gertrude Polinsky, desire to adopt, *has concealed herself* [my emphasis] so that the ordinary process of law cannot be served upon her within the State of Missouri . . ."

In other words, Joey was legally adopted, but without consent of his birth mother, my Aunt Rose. She had "concealed herself."

My Aunt Rose did not want to be found to consent to her son's adoption. Joey's birth father, Edward, had remarried by the time Joey's adoption was completed. In Edward's obituary, I found that he was married to his second wife for fifty-five years and had two more sons with her, Maurice and another Joseph, as well as five grandchildren, and was a warm and pleasant man. No one in his second family had heard of the first Joey.

• • •

The Sanders family on one of our Memorial Day visits to the Cass County cemeteries. I'm on the far left, next to Sharon Simeon. Maurice and Marshall H. Sanders Jr. stand on either side of their children and grandchildren. Courtesy of Maurice Sanders.

After Marshall placed flowers on his parents' gravestones, he turned to me and said, "Well, what would you like to do?"

Marshall knew I wanted to drive to Brownsville Street and introduce myself to Vincent McGee, the man who lived in the house where Aunt Rose had lived. Living in the same house meant that he was in daily contact with the proofs of her existence, the material things I longed to see and touch. I had anticipated meeting and talking with Vincent for over a year, and because this meeting meant so much to me, I had planned to tread carefully in my approach. The house had been Vincent's home practically his whole life—maybe his entire life—while I was only just discovering my aunt and her life.

I had spent almost two years praying and begging for clues that could lead me to know my Aunt Rose. Maybe because her place in my family constellation is a gaping hole and I yearned for kinship with her, I wanted to know more about Aunt Rose than can be known about another person: I wanted to know her thoughts. What did she think about as she fell asleep? What kept her hands busy during the long Michigan winter nights? What occupied her mind as she looked out her window at the trees along the shores of Paradise Lake?

Looking out those same windows now was Vincent McGee, a man who may have held the answers to some of my questions. For me, Vincent was the proscenium before a curtain that refused to rise on my Aunt Rose's life.

But for Vincent, who was I? Was I just a slightly annoying person researching his family because they were somehow connected to an aunt I'd never met?

I had found Vincent's name by searching on the internet for the Brownsville Street address typed on Aunt Rose's death certificate, while at the same time searching for and cross-checking more information about Margaret Davis and Ann McGee. These were the two women whose names were on Aunt Rose's final account and assigning residue papers, the women to whom she'd left her house and all remaining personal property.

There are dozens of businesses run through the internet for the purpose of finding people: findpeoplesearch.com, publicrecordsearcher.com, truthfinder.com, checkmate.com, seekverify.com, intellius.com, and spokeo.com, to name a few. I could fill this page with publicly available ways to find people, and there must be millions of people doing it along with me. Still, I feel very uncomfortable about searching for people on the internet.

And yet: Don't journalists do this all the time? Hadn't I wanted to be a journalist when I was growing up?

Spokeo.com provides the last names of all of the people who have ever lived at a particular address. By checking my own name, I found that it was not completely accurate. But it was a start. After a lot of trial and error, I found contact information for the people living at Aunt Rose's former address on Brownsville Street.

Yet, once I found the information, I had trouble finding the nerve to use it. The ethical problem for me was: How would my sleuthing feel to the person I was looking for? Did they want to be found?

Months had gone by since then, and now here I was with Marshall and Sharon accompanying me to knock on the door of Aunt Rose's final home, to hopefully meet Vincent. They knew how much I wanted to talk to Vincent and how reluctant I was to actually try. But this was my chance.

"I'm ready to try to meet Vincent," I said to Marshall.

On the lake side of Brownsville Street, you can't see any houses, just the beginnings of dirt driveways. By this point, I'd driven down Brownsville Street several times, trying to gaze down the drives to determine which might lead to the house Aunt Rose had lived in. I'd looked at Google's satellite views, and I'd searched the address on Zillow. I wasn't positive, but I was pretty sure I knew which dirt road led to Aunt Rose's last address. I told Marshall and Sharon that I would lead the way, with them following in their car.

Just as I went to get into my Honda Odyssey, I saw that the car doors were locked and that my keys were sitting on the front passenger seat. I mumbled, "Oh darn." Seeing my distress, Sharon walked over, assessed the situation, and reached into the open window to unlock the door. This immediately set off the car alarm. An excruciatingly loud honking continued even after I opened all of the doors, started the engine, turned the car off, and started it again.

The cemetery we were parked in was on a rural, residential street. There were homes nearby. Out of the corner of my eye, I saw window shades rise as I struggled to figure out how to turn the alarm off. I fished around in the glove compartment for the car's manual, which was no help. Even though this was not the first time this had happened to me, I couldn't—and still can't—remember for my life how to silence the blaring alarm. We were all beginning to get agitated and annoyed, and I was embarrassed on top of that. But finally, after about ten minutes, the alarm stopped on its own.

With a huge sigh of relief, I began the short drive to Brownsville Street. I was too flustered to lead the way, so Marshall pulled his car ahead of mine. When we got to the right drive, I signaled him to turn in and followed. Even though the house was hidden from the road, the drive was not long. Marshall and Sharon got out of their car to approach Vincent's house, but when I opened my car door to hop out to join them, the alarm began to blare again.

After waiting for months for this meeting, endlessly replaying the words I wanted to use to introduce myself to Vincent, I could not believe this was happening. I dived back into the car and backed out of the driveway at breakneck speed. I saw Marshall back out too, and we drove up the road about a quarter mile. I drove onto a pullout on the dirt road and turned off the car, overwhelmed with exasperation, embarrassment, and confusion.

The horn stopped again, finally. The three of us got out of our cars to talk. Marshall told me that someone had come out of the house as we were backing out of the driveway. I wanted to go back, so I decided I would leave the car running in the driveway when we returned to the house so that the alarm wouldn't go off again. We both made a U-turn with our cars, and this time I led and Marshall followed. I pulled in, almost to the house, and there was Vincent and his fifteen-year-old son, Vinny (I knew him right away, as I'd seen photos of him on Facebook). Both of them had very guarded, surprised looks. I left my car with the engine running and opened the door. The deafening, blaring horn started up again. By this point, Marshall had parked his car behind me in the narrow driveway. There was no going back at this point. I had to go introduce myself to Vincent McGee.

Vincent and Vinny had walked several yards down the drive toward the cars and were waiting warily to find out what this was all about. My car horn was blaring so loudly that I had to scream just to say hello. The longer I stood there trying to say something, the more I felt I'd completely blown—utterly destroyed—this opportunity to find out what the McGees knew of Aunt Rose.

Thank God Marshall and Sharon were not as flustered. Sharon introduced us and asked enough questions to get the conversation going. Vincent confirmed that he and his teenage son lived in the house on Brownsville Street that had been Aunt Rose's last address—the home I believed she lived in for many years. The house she left to Margaret Davis and Ann McGee, who were, Vincent confirmed, his grandmother and mother. Four generations of Vincent's family had by now lived in the Brownsville house that Aunt Rose had lived in for many years.

This was the confirmation I had been waiting for. I was standing with the descendants of Aunt Rose's Vandalia family. In that moment, I imagined meeting her closest friends and speaking to them about her. That is, if it weren't for the car alarm screaming behind me.

While the horn blew, I found out that Vincent had been eight when Aunt Rose died and that he barely remembered her. "I believe she was a friend of my grandmother, Margaret Davis," Vincent said. He gestured to the west and continued, "I believe she owned everything from here up to the next road, where the horses are." He explained that old Mr. Bell owned the lakefront property going the other way. He had died the year prior at age ninety-one, while his wife, Martha Bell, had died in 2000. They had been Aunt Rose's neighbors for many years.

Finally, the horn went quiet and we could speak in normal voices. We told Vincent that we'd just come from visiting the cemeteries. I said that I noticed my Aunt Rose was buried next to Yaffee McGee.

"My grandfather," Vincent filled in.

This led into a question that Marshall had on his mind: "Vincent, do you know Bill Vaughn?"

Mr. Vaughn, the sexton of the cemeteries, the man who had known where Aunt Rose was buried because he had dug her grave, was, we learned, Vincent's father. In fact,

Mr. Vaughn had passed on the care of the cemeteries to Vincent, and Vincent had passed the mowing on to Vinny. All the freshly mown cemeteries we'd just visited had been cared for by the fifteen-year-old standing in front of us. Vincent told us that although his mother was ill, he had just spoken to her that morning. She lived a couple of hours away. He promised to contact her to ask her to reach out to me. We exchanged cell phone numbers.

There were so many more questions to ask, but we were all exhausted from the shock and annoyance of the horn blasts. After not more than fifteen minutes, we said goodbye. When I opened the car door to leave, the alarm went off again, and I drove down Brownsville Street mortified, laughing to keep away the tears. After all, I'd made my first encounter with Vincent McGee, the grandson of Aunt Rose's good friend Margaret.

I received one very brief email from Vincent's mother in which she confirmed she had photos, somewhere, of Aunt Rose. After that, neither Vincent nor his mother responded to any of my attempts to contact them.

I wonder, sometimes, whether their unwillingness to speak with me further is an attempt to honor Aunt Rose's wishes—whether my being a Kinberg, from the family that disowned her, is the reason they've decided to keep the details of her life concealed.

Finding people who might have known my Aunt Rose and her husband, Mr. Arnwine, drove me out of the normally small bubble of my daily life. I put a note on my desk: "Interview her friends." This was not an easy task, as Aunt Rose was born in 1908 and died in 1982. Still, the search became my mission. I wrote and messaged and called and slowly found a web of strangers to support me. I again returned to the cemetery to try to find out more about her neighbors, the people she was buried among.

The grave to the left of Aunt Rose's belongs to Yaffee McGee, Vincent's grandfather and the first husband of Aunt Rose's friend Margaret, the woman to whom she willed her house. Aunt Rose's small home, hidden down a dirt driveway off of Brownsville Street, was hers for forty years. Margaret, who is buried in another county near her birth family, died a few years after Aunt Rose, in 1987; Yaffee lived until 2003. Yaffee's grave marker identifies him as an army veteran.

I imagine that Aunt Rose met Yaffee and Margaret McGee in the first years she lived on Paradise Lake. The McGees were newlyweds in 1943, the year Mr. Arnwine and his friends bought the property on Paradise Lake. The McGees had been married in nearby Battle Creek, Michigan, even though Yaffee was from Ohio and, at the time of their wedding, during World War II, was a US Army soldier stationed in New Bedford, Massachusetts.

On the McGees' marriage certificate, "white" is typed into the blanks asking for the applicants' "color." But "white" is crossed through and "black" is handwritten above for both Yaffee and Margaret. It is likely that the clerk typing the certificate looked at the soldier and his fiancée and coded them as white. Sometime between then and when the marriage certificate was uploaded to the internet, the correction was made.

Yaffee's racial designation on his marriage certificate mattered: His US Army registration listed him as Black, and therefore he would be serving in a Black unit in our country's segregated military.

When I found the McGees' marriage certificate, with its crossed-out and changed racial designations, I thought I might be on to something important about Aunt Rose's connection to Margaret. In the 1940 US census, Aunt Rose, a daughter of European Ashkenazi Jewish immigrants, had been designated by the government as "Negro" presumably because of her residence in a segregated Black Chicago neighborhood. In Vandalia, Aunt Rose found other people whose racial designations shifted depending on local custom, along with the impulse of whoever was filling in the blanks.

Aunt Rose's new friend Margaret Roberts McGee was from a family of several generations of Ohio and Michigan farmers. She had white European-born grandmothers on both sides of her family. When these women married free, mixed-race men before the Civil War, their families were alternately listed on census forms as "Black" or "mulatto" in rural areas where everyone else on the census page was listed as "white." In the 1850 census of "free inhabitants" of Ohio (enslaved people were not counted by the US census until the first census after the Civil War, in 1870), Margaret's paternal great-grandparents were marked mulatto, even though her great-grandmother was white and born in Germany. Twenty years later, in the 1870 census, which includes Margaret's maternal grandparents, the *M* (mulatto) was crossed out, and *W* (white) was written above it to match all the *W*'s on the rest of the page.

Because of legal segregation in the United States until the Civil Rights Act of 1964, all people living here were forced by the government to be assigned a race or color. Beginning in 1870, the first census after the Civil War, census takers were instructed to never leave the race or color question blank. This was the rule until 1960, when the census transitioned to allowing people to self-identify their race. Since the Civil Rights Act of 1964, which prohibited discrimination based on race, racial data has continued to be collected. According to the US Census Bureau, this is "to promote equal employment opportunities and to assess racial disparities in health and environmental risks."

The instructions for the 1870 census takers read: "It must not be assumed that, where nothing is written in [column 6, 'Color'] 'White' is to be understood. The column is always to be filled. Be particularly careful in reporting the class Mulatto. The word is here generic, and includes quadroons, octoroons, and all persons having any *perceptible* [my emphasis] trace of African blood."

Later, the instructions to census takers in 1930 read: "A person of mixed White and Negro blood was to be returned as Negro, no matter how small the percentage of Negro blood; someone part Indian and part Negro also was to be listed as Negro unless the Indian blood predominated and the person was *generally accepted* [my emphasis] as an Indian in the community."

In 1940, the instructions were even more explicit but still relied on the determination of the census taker (rather than self-reporting, which is the practice in the twenty-first century):

> A person of mixed white and Negro blood should be returned as a Negro, no matter how small the percentage of Negro blood. Both black and mulatto persons are to be returned as Negroes, without distinction. A person of mixed Indian and Negro blood should be returned as a Negro, unless the Indian blood very definitely predominates and he is universally accepted in the community as an Indian. . . . Any mixture of white and nonwhite should be reported according to the nonwhite parent. Mixtures of nonwhite races should be reported according to the race of the father, except that Negro-Indian should be reported as Negro.

There are no such instructions on filling in death certificates: The race or color is filled in by whoever the informant happens to be, usually a family member or funeral home worker. On my grandfather's 1934 Texas death certificate, "Jew" is typed in the space for "race or color." When I saw the word "Jew" on that document, I felt a powerful mix of connection and pride, as well as sadness and fear. In Texas in 1934, my grandfather's racial designation was "Jew," even though in all legal cases, Ashkenazi Jews were ruled as white (though Syrian Jews were not). My grandfather wouldn't have argued with this assignation. He was proud of his heritage. But I wonder how and why the Texan filling out the form decided that "Jew" was my grandfather's race.

On her death certificate, Aunt Rose listed herself as white (she provided information for her death certificate in advance). By this time, she had already paid for a burial plot in a historic Black cemetery. However, she had not arranged for a headstone to mark her presence there.

Rosella Coker Wade is also buried in the Calvin Community Chapel Cemetery, not far from Aunt Rose's burial plot. In an oral history recorded by a white volunteer in 1978, ninety-year-old Ms. Wade, born into some of the oldest families in Cass County, referred to people of the past, and people outside of her family, as the "colored people" or the "whites." Her storytelling didn't indicate whether she personally identified with either race until the interviewer pressed her about the Calvin Community Chapel:

Interviewer: Were . . . any white people members of your church?

Rosella Coker Wade: No, well, of course some of them are mixed with white, but no white, no pure white.

When she passed away in 1995 at the age of 103, Ms. Wade was the oldest living descendant of Ezekiel Anderson (1788–1851), a Native American man who had, as a child, witnessed the massacre of his whole village, including his family, by white settlers. He survived the attack and was taken by a white man to South Carolina, where he was raised. After serving in the war of 1812 under Andrew Jackson, Ezekiel Anderson married a woman of mixed African and white heritage and together they were classified as "colored" rather than "Indian" in the 1820 US census. In 1838, all of the Native Americans living in their area of Illinois were forced into a westward death march. Ezekiel Anderson and his wife, classified not as "Indian" but as "colored," were not forced into the march. Instead, they packed up and moved to Cass County, Michigan, where they farmed and raised their many children and now have hundreds of descendants. According to an article written in 1995 by Ruth Anderson Walker, one of Ezekiel Anderson's descendants born in Vandalia, "This mistake in the racial designation [on the US census] of Ezekiel Anderson proved to be advantageous for him. Indians were feared and hated at that time, while colored people were considered harmless."

When I mentioned Ezekiel Anderson to Marshall, he said, "Why, I think Ruth Walker who wrote all that is still alive." Ms. Walker's parents—like Marshall's parents, Rosella Coker Wade, and my Aunt Rose—are buried in Calvin Community Chapel Cemetery. Marshall had been trying for five years to connect me with some local elders who might have known Aunt Rose and Mr. Arnwine. He now told me he would try to contact Ms. Walker.

Ms. Walker, in her nineties, was still living in southwest Michigan. I called her on April 29, 2021, and, finally, I had someone on the line who knew my aunt and her husband. Someone with stories to tell: Zeb, as she called him, had sold them a car that Ms. Walker hated; Aunt Rose had once been in a car accident with Ms. Walker's brother; a good friend of Aunt Rose's attended the same Church of God as Ms. Walker and her mother.

From Ms. Walker I learned that Mr. Arnwine was very light-skinned—from a distance, you might think he was white, she told me. Ms. Walker knew—but didn't know—that Aunt Rose was Jewish. "I thought Arnwine was a Jewish-sounding name," Ms. Walker said, "and I never saw Rose in church." But she didn't remember discussing this with anyone. She told me she remembered Aunt Rose as a lonely person, and that she didn't know any other Jewish people in the community besides Aunt Rose.

The population of Cass County grew substantially in the years right after Aunt Rose and Mr. Arnwine moved to the community. Paradise Lake blossomed as a Black resort in the 1940s and 1950s, an escape for urban families weary of the segregation and racism they had to endure in the cities where they lived, including Chicago, Detroit, and Indianapolis. The north shore of the lake had a hotel, cottages for rent, and places to eat and drink, and thousands of African Americans came to vacation each summer. Sections of the north shore were purchased and platted for new cottages.

I asked Marshall how people in the community talked about race during these years, when Aunt Rose and Mr. Arnwine were new in the community. He was born in 1940 and has vivid memories of his childhood summers in Vandalia.

A highlight of every summer was the bush meeting (also called the grove meeting) in the woods behind the Stone Church. It was a revival, a reunion, a picnic, and a whole community gathering. Marshall shared a cherished photo from the 1945 bush meeting. The picture was so fuzzy that I couldn't clearly identify anyone, but I looked deeply into each face, wondering whether Aunt Rose took part in this all-community event. Was that her seated on the bottom row, second from right? The thought gave me joy.

Marshall's stories revealed both the protected nature of the area and how the era's racial tensions seeped in:

> In 1949 I was not thinking about race. At the age of 8, this was not in my consciousness. The children at the Vandalia K–8 school we knew were black and white. In retrospect it did not appear the students grouped together by race. But a couple memories do stand out.

In the early 1950s one summer several of us formed a "Boys Club" on the second level of the barn. The only way to access the second level was using a ladder from the outside to reach a small door opening. One of the boys from Chicago, visiting his grandparents, did not want the "white boys" to come up the ladder and enter the club. Though at the time I did not totally understand the reason why, it was me who told my two white friends they could not come up the ladder. I saw a confused, hurt, and disappointed look on their faces as they descended the ladder and left the yard. I always regretted this action on my part.

Another Vandalia incident (year unknown) happened to me while riding my bike in downtown Vandalia. An adult white man approached me angrily, asking "Where is Odie?" I said I did not know. He said Odie had slapped his daughter. He walked away saying, "All of you stick together," and that he would find Odie. Odie was a black boy who I knew but did not associate with. I never heard any more about the incident.

Marshall's childhood remembrances are of a bruised innocence. They are stories of the place Aunt Rose lived and the people she lived among, his memories of her friends and the people she rests among in Calvin Community Chapel Cemetery.

Ruth Anderson Walker was born in Vandalia in 1930. She and her husband published a newspaper, motivated, she told me, by the fact that the other papers didn't adequately cover the Black community. Ms. Walker has also written about

Grove Meeting, Vandalia, 1945. Courtesy of Marshall H. Sanders Jr.

experiencing World War II as a teenager in high school in southwest Michigan during the years Aunt Rose lived there. The war in Europe affected everyone, Ms. Walker wrote. Even in tiny, out-of-the-way Vandalia, rationing and blackouts after dark were carefully observed in support of the war effort. Although Aunt Rose and Ms. Walker, the youngest of ten children, were almost a generation apart in age, both had brothers who registered to serve in the military. Rose's baby brother Leonard was sent to the South Pacific; the war ended before Ms. Walker's brother was deployed.

Ms. Walker's mother, Emmaline—married at age sixteen in 1904—was the same age as Aunt Rose's mother, who also married young and had a large family. Although she was widowed in 1925, my Aunt Rose's mother was known in the neighborhood as someone who was always cooking and would readily feed a hungry neighborhood kid.

Trying to get a fuller picture of Aunt Rose, I peppered Ms. Walker with questions: "What do you remember about Rose Arnwine?" I implored. "Anything at all will help me get a sense of who she was."

"She cooked," Ms. Walker told me. "She traded recipes with her friends. And she helped Zeb run the barbecue business." Ms. Walker added with chagrin, "They had 'Zeb's Bar-B-Q' brightly painted on the side of their car." When the Walkers bought Mr. Arnwine's car, the advertisement was still on the car, which was very irritating to Ms. Walker.

The barbeque business? When Ms. Walker told me that Mr. Arnwine and Aunt Rose sold barbecue in Vandalia, my picture of Aunt Rose's life changed shape. I developed a revised "How did Aunt Rose and Mr. Arnwine meet?" hypothesis. Based on my own life as an activist on the left, I had hoped they met at a St. Louis Unemployment Council rally organized by the Workers Alliance, as I described in an earlier chapter. Although most of the interracial couples from the 1930s about whom I'd read had met through the Communist Party and related organizing, that story doesn't fit well with anything else in my family history. Something more grounded in the lives of striving small business owners could be closer to the truth. Perhaps sometime in the 1930s, Aunt Rose was behind a counter when Mr. Arnwine came in to look at some hardware for a barbecue pit.

My father worked at Kinberg Hardware, and his sister Rose might have worked there, or possibly at another shop nearby. The only person in the Kinberg family able to offer employment, my Great-Uncle Jack, opened a hardware store in St. Louis, Missouri, on Franklin Ave, in 1921 and didn't shut its doors until a fire in November of 1965. Great-Uncle Jack helped my father's family after 1925, when my grandfather Joseph died and left seven children with a mother who didn't speak English and could not read or write.

In this scenario, Mr. Arnwine is already the entrepreneur I know he later became. As he looks around the store, he's thinking and planning. One of the few things he's carried with him from Muskogee, Oklahoma, is the family barbecue sauce recipe. If he could just set up somewhere, he'd be in business. When he comes into Kinberg Hardware, Rose can tell he has a plan in mind. He's looking to the future; he's not looking back. Rose is immediately drawn to Mr. Arnwine and his plans, which seem tangible, possible. Maybe he talks Great-Uncle Jack into selling him a barrel and some grates on time, so he has to come in every so often and make payments. Rose and he get to talking over the next few months. His plan is working. Before too long, they leave for Chicago with ideas about cooking and selling barbecue.

In the 1940s, Southern-style barbecue businesses were opening all over the Black neighborhoods in Chicago. Argia B. Collins and his five entrepreneurial brothers operated successful rib joints across Chicago's South Side, where their specialty was a spicy mumbo sauce.

"Inspired by his southern roots, Collins crafted his own tantalizing new sauce—sweet, tangy, savory, sublime!" says the website of Argia B's Mumbo Sauce.

"DC mambo sauce" is also the term for a tangy, spicy sauce that many Washington, DC, locals consider to be the flavor of their city. But as a September 13, 2013, *Washington Post* headline about the settlement of a trademark dispute describes it, the mambo sauce is "the taste of D.C., but in the eyes of the law its home is Chicago."

Mr. Arnwine also had a mambo sauce recipe, an entrepreneurial spirit, and a partner in my Aunt Rose whose family tradition was to find something to sell and make a go of it.

Along with a move to Michigan, perhaps Aunt Rose and Mr. Arnwine developed a plan for a Southern-style barbecue restaurant in the up-and-coming Black resort area on Paradise Lake—what I assume would have been an irresistible, tantalizing idea. Ms. Walker told me that while Zeb handled the meats and deliveries, Aunt Rose cooked. And she kept the books. "She was his guiding light," Ms. Walker said. "She ran the business."

Since I doubted that barbecue was in the cooking repertoire Aunt Rose learned from her immigrant Romanian Jewish mother, I began to wonder about the merger of Mr. Arnwine and Aunt Rose's cooking styles. Oh, what I would have given to be able to see a menu from "Zeb's Bar-B-Q" in Vandalia, 1955, and to watch Aunt Rose and Mr. Arnwine as they cooked together at home and delivered fresh meals in the loudly painted car that advertised "Zeb's Bar-B-Q" across its sides.

After my Aunt Rose and Mr. Arnwine divorced in 1957, he opened a barbecue joint in South Bend, Indiana, just south of the Michigan border, and later, in 1967, he opened Zeb's Bar-B-Q on Thirty-Eighth and Keystone in Indianapolis. That same year, Mr. Arnwine told a reporter from the *Indianapolis Recorder*, the city's Black newspaper (founded in 1895 and still publishing), that his new restaurant would specialize in a sauce made from a recipe that had been in his family for eighty years. "Mr. Arnwine has been offered big money for the formula, but he refuses to sell," the article stated. The secret recipe for Zeb's original mambo sauce is still an internet topic of nostalgic discussion by old-timers from Indianapolis. I gathered from descriptions of Zeb's Bar-B-Q in an online forum that his Haitian ham ribs shoulder, as advertised on the marquee, was similar to what was labeled Oklahoma-style barbecue elsewhere—a combination of Texas-style, slow-cooked, fall-off-the-bone meat with a sweet, tangy Kansas-style sauce.

Now, when I think about Aunt Rose in Vandalia, I feel transported to her kitchen, the smell of smoking barbeque from the yard drifting in amid the steam of boiling potatoes and simmering sweet, spicy sauce. Vandalia might have been a refuge from the daily pressures and indignities of racism, and the kitchen a covert within a covert, but in my mind, sometimes the steam meeting the taut, electric air heralds a storm about to come raging in.

This is a part of the story I haven't wanted to tell.

During my forty-year search for Aunt Rose, I quizzed relatives I barely knew for clues to her life. In the 1990s, I corresponded with an older cousin in Chicago who remembered Aunt Rose coming to her family's Hyde Park apartment—more than once—in the middle of the night. My cousin Hillaine's mother, my Great-Aunt Mary, was the legendary rock of the family—kindhearted and dependable. For the St. Louis Kinbergs, going to Chicago always meant a visit to Great-Aunt Mary.

• • •

Great-Aunt Mary was my grandfather's youngest sister and was only ten years older than Aunt Rose. If I'd had the wherewithal to talk to Great-Aunt Mary about Aunt Rose, I might now know so much more. But here is what I do know based on my conversations with Hillaine: Hillaine told me she remembered, as a child, peeking around a corner while her mother and Rose conferred in the kitchen, Rose crying. With confidence in her childhood perceptions of the situation, Hillaine told me that Rose regretted her decisions to leave her son Joey and to move away with Mr. Arnwine. Her husband beat her, Hillaine said.

Like the very fact of Aunt Rose—the missing aunt I'd never met, whose existence I put aside at age twelve, when I first heard reference to her, to process much later—the fact that she was beaten by her husband was a piece of information I had to tuck away. I couldn't let her status as an outcast—or the information that her husband beat her—define my understanding of my aunt's life. She had crossed the color line when it seemed to me, for our family, to be a mostly unbreachable wall. She'd left St. Louis and not come back. She'd visited Great-Aunt Mary in Chicago, but she always returned to Paradise Lake. I needed to know more about her life's journey, including more about the man with whom she left St. Louis.

With persistence, luck, and the mystery of coincidence, I've accumulated a few stories about Mr. Arnwine. In the spring of 2021, as I was rushing around getting ready to fly down to Florida to visit my older daughter, I got a phone call from a Virginia number I didn't recognize. As is my habit, I answered, "Hello, this is Clare."

Zeb's Bar-B-Q in Indianapolis, Indiana.

The hesitant voice at the other end said, "I didn't expect you to pick up the phone. You've written about my grandmother in Oklahoma." I sat down. It was eight thirty in the morning on April 16. I'd been publishing stories about Aunt Rose and Mr. Arnwine for a year and a half.

The woman on the phone had found the story I'd written about Mr. Arnwine's early life in Muskogee, Oklahoma, and had identified his second wife, Tamah Walker, as her grandmother. Speaking to me was Pastor Gay L. Gray, a writer and teacher offering online spiritual development courses. Pastor Gray's mother was Tamah's daughter from a subsequent marriage after she'd divorced Mr. Arnwine. She had never met her grandmother or Mr. Arnwine, but Pastor Gray has a very keen interest in her family's history.

"Everything you wrote about my grandmother—that her mother was an enrolled Creek freedwoman, that she'd been allotted valuable property when the tribal lands were broken up, that appointed white guardians tried to take away her land, that she had married Zebedee Arnwine in the early 1920s and had a daughter, Rebecca—all is true," she told me. "My Aunt Rebecca, in her nineties, is still living," she said, "and my own extensive research into my very multiracial and complicated genealogy confirms the story you wrote." Somehow, I learned, her family had lost the land with the oil and gas underneath.

Pastor Gray was grateful that, because of my essays, more people would know her family's stories of land theft, but she also had more to say about Mr. Arnwine. Tamah Walker, she went on to tell me, had saved in a trunk a set of blood-stained clothes, her grandmother's evidence that Mr. Arnwine, her husband, had beaten her in a dispute over the deed to the land allotment. Mr. Arnwine was not a good memory in her family. Pastor Gray wasn't surprised that he'd moved on to marry a white woman and that he had beaten her, too.

"He was very bright," she told me, explaining she meant very light-skinned, in case I didn't understand her meaning. From what she'd understood about him, Mr. Arnwine didn't have a place in the world where he felt at home, or that he could call his own.

I continued to search for more on Mr. Arnwine; I couldn't let the knowledge of his violence toward Aunt Rose define him or overshadow his ambitious and unconventional life. My intention for this book about Aunt Rose and Mr. Arnwine was to find the stories behind the stories.

Finally, my search uncovered a story that was so pertinent that I could only imagine it was written for me personally to find. It was a story of an older Mr. Arnwine, a man who had, for a while anyway, found a place where he was remembered for his charm and generosity. This story about Mr. Arnwine was written in 1982 by Mark Vittert in his occasional newspaper column in the *St. Louis Business Journal*, which he cofounded. Though I hadn't heard of Vittert prior to finding this column, Vittert was a media entrepreneur from St. Louis who had been a part owner of the *Riverfront Times*, St. Louis's leading weekly, and his company, Lee Enterprises, was an owner of the *St. Louis Post-Dispatch*. To express the good fortune of finding this touching anecdotal story about Mr. Arnwine published in a St. Louis newspaper, I have included the full column:

Mark Vittert's Reflections:
Thanksgiving with Mambo Sauce

In those days I didn't have a credit card and I carried only a few bucks with me at any time. It was Thanksgiving night in 1970 and I was on my way out for dinner. It turned out later that everyone at our Indianapolis company had thought somebody else had invited me over. So I found myself without an invitation, going out to eat alone. I had all of four dollars with me.

As I walked into a smorgasbord, the sign at the front door said, "Thanksgiving Special $5.95." At that moment my hunger was only surpassed by how lonely I felt.

I went to a pay phone and called home to St. Louis. The family was having a big dinner with lots of friends. Mom told me how much everyone missed me and that she hoped I was having a good time. Frankly, I blinked twice and told her that I was invited to a friend's home for Thanksgiving and that it would be warm and friendly and fun.

As we said goodbye, I found myself standing on Meridian Street with four dollars and nowhere to go.

I tried a couple of more nice restaurants, but my four dollars just wasn't going to get me farther than the cranberry sauce. And then I saw "ZEBS." It was a big, neon sign over a converted gasoline station. It said "ZEBS" with "Original MAMBO sauce." Original mambo sauce—I just had to see what this was.

It was stone empty inside. The smell of ribs was inviting and I yielded to a Thanksgiving dinner of barbecue and potato salad—if I could afford it.

Zeb was standing behind the counter. About 60 years old with a look that reminded me of a relaxed Sonny Liston stare.

I said "Mr. Zeb, if that's who you are, I've got four dollars and only four dollars for my Thanksgiving dinner. Give me whatever four dollars can buy."

He scowled. "Is this your holiday night, out here all alone?"

"Yep."

He stepped from behind the counter and went over and locked the front door. As he turned down toward me, he had softened. He said, "Young fella, let's go in the back and really have ourselves a Thanksgiving dinner. My wife died last summer and I'm alone too."

Boy, did we have a feast. Zeb and I became good friends that year.

The next year, once again I found myself in Indianapolis for Thanksgiving. After everyone found out that no one had invited me out the year before, I was besieged with invitations for grand evenings all over town. But I already had plans.

Zeb and I had our second Thanksgiving dinner together.

Not long after Mark Vittert's second Thanksgiving with him, Mr. Arnwine sold the restaurant and moved back to Chicago. In November of 1976, Mr. Arnwine died and was buried in an unmarked grave in Burr Oak Cemetery in Alsip, Illinois, just outside of Chicago. Burr Oak is also the resting place of Emmett Till and his family. On a trip to Chicago in June 2021, my daughter and I paid respects to both of them.

6

WHERE IS MY PLACE? WHO ARE MY PEOPLE?

All who I love are of my people. It is not simple.
—Audre Lorde, 1962, quoted in *Survival Is a Promise*

Aunt Rose and Mr. Arnwine's divorce papers in 1957 assigned Aunt Rose sole ownership of the land on Paradise Lake. Mr. Arnwine, the descendant of enslaved people and farmers, took his portable skills—cooking and entrepreneurship—and moved to South Bend, then Indianapolis, then back to Chicago. He became an urban wanderer, or maybe that is just how I understand it from my perch as the descendant of wandering Jews. My Aunt Rose, daughter of immigrant Jewish junk dealers, stayed put in a small community of Black farmers and became a jobber, not of hardware and scrap metal like her father and brother but of lakeside acre plots in a subdivision she named Arnwine Shores. She also worked as a nurse's aide in a hospital in South Bend. She was making ends meet.

Rose's first grandson was born the year of her divorce. By then, Rose had been separated from the St. Louis Kinberg family for two decades. (I was two in 1957.) As she and her siblings reached midlife, their cleavage was a tired habit, difficult to change. I think of family members I haven't seen in decades; my daughters barely know them. Though I feel alienated from family members who seem to accept racism in the way of my father, and I want to protect my children from them, the loss of family is painful, too.

The final picture I found of Aunt Rose showed up in a scrapbook of my mother's. The picture of two women standing in a backyard is only labeled with a date, but I know the woman on the right holding a handbag is my Great-Aunt Mary. Great-Aunt Mary was a constant in my family constellation. But I also now recognize the unnamed woman on the left as my Aunt Rose. The photo was alone on a page of a scrapbook among pages of other photos taken by my father. The back is dated July 14, 1957. I believe my father took the picture, and that is why my mother had it in a scrapbook. In the photo, Aunt Rose is fifty years old, her formerly luminous eyes—captured in the picture from the 1920s—narrowed, sunken behind swollen lids. Aunt Rose looks uncomfortable, wary, and weary as she looks directly at the photographer, my father. Almost seventy years later, she now seems to peer out at me. I imagine she has just decisively told my father she is staying put in Vandalia. As he is leaving, he snaps a photo. I am the inheritor of this captured moment.

Rose divorced at age fifty, an age when, in ways peculiar to midlife, both looking back and looking forward occupy our minds. "What now?" she might have asked herself. I've been there.

When my daughters were young children, Patti and I were close to fifty, and we pursued moving back to St. Louis. We looked for jobs in St. Louis, but when Patti found a job

Aunt Rose on the left and Great-Aunt Mary on the right, dated July 14, 1957, in my mother's handwriting.

nearby in Michigan, we had to close the St. Louis door for twenty more years. We raised our daughters in a community where we had no relatives.

If Aunt Rose had returned to St. Louis at fifty, after her divorce, her family would have had to shift their relationships, face the betrayal, and perhaps speak about how racism had broken the family. That did not happen. Aunt Rose chose to continue her life on the shore of Paradise Lake. Whatever she learned about living in a community of God-fearing, rural African Americans died with her, and because of the betrayal, that knowledge was denied to me. Aunt Rose kept to herself and traded recipes with her friends. They took care of her in her final illness. She is buried among them.

I think I understand her decision to stay in Vandalia, at least part of it. Since Patti and I and the girls left Oregon in 2003, we have lived in either mixed-race or majority-Black neighborhoods and school districts. For many years, it was "for the kids." We wanted them to have opportunities to be in Black community.

Our adult children live on their own now, but Patti and I still choose to live in a Black-majority neighborhood. Because we are an interracial family in a segregated society, our life is with Black people. I know that wherever there are not Black people, or wherever they are only a very small proportion of the population, racism is the cause. Historic, current, systemic, micro, overt, or subtle, anti-Black racism is behind social segregation. We don't escape the racism by living in a Black community—no one does—but sharing roads and stores, stoplights and utilities, and schools and polling places creates something of familiarity and intimacy for our family. Whether or not she would have used these words, Aunt Rose's life choices defied our country's racism. She stayed in Vandalia. Our lives with Black people create a kinship between Aunt Rose and me outside of time, and although I am drawn to know her because of our birth family relationship, our kinship is not only tribal.

In 1960, Aunt Rose platted her property on the south shore of Paradise Lake into one-acre plots, planning a subdivision for new families moving to Cass County and families wanting to summer at the resort area "reserved for colored people."

However, just as her planned lakeside subdivision was getting off the ground, the United States passed the landmark 1964 Civil Rights Act, which outlawed racial segregation in accommodations and entertainments. After 1964, African Americans had less need to seek out their own resorts. The community on Paradise Lake stopped growing. After that, Aunt Rose's plots were not as valuable as, I imagine, she hoped.

Through the rise and fall of Vandalia's resort era, the south shore of Paradise Lake remained much the same. Aunt Rose's neighbors were deeply religious, family-oriented farmers, teachers, and small business owners. She was a woman alone now, neither a descendant of the old families nor a resort-era newcomer.

Aunt Rose's property extended to the shore of Paradise Lake, but she didn't have a dock or a boat from which to fish. Her driveway intersected with the driveway of Sister Julia Ash, who was active in the Church of God, but Rose did not attend that church. Another family of neighbors, the Weatherspoons, were members of the Church of God. The Weatherspoon children were expected, one told me, to help their neighbors, and one of them remembers mowing Aunt Rose's lawn. "Ms. Arnwine was quiet and reserved," he told me.

He asked his brothers and sisters what they remembered of Rose Arnwine. "She was independent and private, kind and businesslike," he reported back to me. Aunt Rose had found a place to be, a covert, yet she too remained hidden.

Finding little bits and pieces of Aunt Rose's life has been solitary work; I've been alone with shadows, trying to mold them into stories. When I started writing this story about my Aunt Rose, I didn't know what I was looking for, yet there seemed to be meaning in each discovery.

When my father died in 1975, my unknown Aunt Rose was the same age I am now. If she was at my father's funeral, no one acknowledged her. I was twenty then, numb and indifferent to the grief felt by my father's three sisters who were there. Rather than feeling anything during the funeral, I was thinking: "Hallelujah, another racist gone." Cold, I know—an emotional chilliness has long traveled with me, bound up with my abhorrence of racism.

Not long after he died, I began to have a recurring dream about my father. In the dream, I was in a parking lot, running or hiding, scared and confused. My father then appeared, sitting in a wheelchair. He was middle-aged, a little younger than when he died at age sixty-four. He couldn't move, but he exuded strength. He was in the parking lot to look out for me, I somehow knew, and I trusted him. His presence protected me, and I would wake from these dreams filled with gratitude, a feeling that dissipated as soon as I began to think.

I still have never cried for him; our love had ruptured many years before his death.

While deep into the writing of this story, exploring how to tell it, how to convey what the pieces of Aunt Rose and Mr. Arnwine's lives meant to me, a chance encounter opened another window. I attended a public lecture on the twelfth-century Jewish philosopher Maimonides given by a learned family friend. When my friend delineated Maimonides's process for having necessary conversations about hurt, of moving forward, with love, after damage to your relationship, he seemed to be talking directly to me.

The lecture translated into everyday English Maimonides's advice on criticizing a friend's or family member's behavior. The advice sounded like a modern self-help book, which I don't normally read; my nature is to look for social solutions, not personal ones. Yet the wisdom of Maimonides spoke to me.

The instructions first begin with naming the hurt; they advise not to ignore or bury it. If a friend (or family member) does damage, the mitzvah, according to Maimonides, is to enable the person to repair the hurt. Ask them: Why did you do this? Then, if there is sincere regret and the person asks forgiveness, they should be forgiven. If there is no regret, go back to the person again and again, and then eventually move on if they do not grow to regret the hurt they have caused. However, do not shame the wrongdoer, as this does not help.

As I wrote this book, I tried to have a conversation with my father, who died a half century ago. The deeper I got into the story of his sister Rose, the closer I got to naming the damage caused by my father's racism and the hurt I feel because my father, rather than being repelled by racial prejudice, adopted the racist's ugly ways. Writing this story helped me name the hurt: the perpetration of racism.

My intention to absolutely reject the racism I grew up with has also included jettisoning much of the biblical and prophetic texts that form the backbone of Jewish tradition. The texts are so peppered with racism and misogyny as to be, it seemed to me, irredeemable. As a parent and teacher, I often invented new stories based on the biblical ones—stories that included active and named women, for example, and that excluded the God-directed genocide of non-Israelite tribes. I balked at telling my kids what was really written on the parchment of the ancient texts.

But as I tell my family's story, I'm learning to approach my inheritances, personal and communal, in a new way. Dr. Judith Plaskow, a contemporary Jewish feminist theologian, urges me to articulate the words accurately, even if they sound terrible. In her essay "Preaching Against the Text," Plaskow writes, "Remaining silent about the negative aspects of tradition not only leaves them to do their work in the world, it also deprives us of an important spiritual resource." Plaskow concludes, "I do not believe that we have any choice other than to make choices about what we accept and repudiate in tradition. But we do have a choice as to whether we leave the negative to do its silent, poisonous work like an old family secret, or whether we turn and grapple with [its] ambiguity and ugliness, and force [it] to yield up meaning. Confronting the hard places in tradition and in our lives is neither comfortable nor easy."

In Deuteronomy, the last book of the Torah, it is written that Moses says, "In the cities of the nations the Lord your

God is giving you as an inheritance, do not leave alive anything that breathes. Completely destroy them—the Hittites, Amorites, Canaanites, Perizzites, Hivites, and Jebusites—as the Lord your God has commanded you" (Deuteronomy 20:17). When I began teaching religious school—seventh graders at United Hebrew in St. Louis in the 1980s—I would not read this text to my students, but rather I would assign my students to research the ancient peoples the Israelites lived among. Who were the Hittites, the Amorites, and the Canaanites? Now I ask: What more can I learn from the revulsion I feel when reading these words? As I write my family's history, can I somehow repair the damage?

Biblical language has also helped me as I have encountered the landscapes of Aunt Rose's covert, her *mistor*, in southwest Michigan. Underneath Aunt Rose's imagined life, the Torah stories rise and take new shape. I've read what I've experienced, and what I imagine the Arnwines and Aunt Rose experienced, into the ancient landscape. The Torah stories of the land between the Jordan River and the Mediterranean Sea become the stories of Texas and Oklahoma, and of the land between the Great Lakes.

One hundred and fifty years ago, a *makom*, a region, on which the ancient Caddo people had lived for thousands of years—what we now call Cherokee County, Texas, the place where Mr. Arnwine's forebears had been enslaved—was willed to the women and their families whom Albartis Arnwine had enslaved, and then the land was stolen from them. In the heart of the *makom* where the Caddo people lived, there is a monument to the folkloric "weeping Mary," the inconsolable, formerly enslaved woman who'd been swindled out of her land by a white man in a story similar to the Arnwines' and to thousands of others.

Fifty years after the Civil War, Zebedee Arnwine married, then bloodied, Tamah Walker, descendant of the Creek Freedmen, who had struggled all of her life to maintain control of her Oklahoma land allotment. In Texas, Oklahoma, and Michigan, the lands the Arnwines struggled over had been stolen from the Caddo, from the Choctaw, Chickasaw, Muscogee, Cherokee, and Seminole, from the Potawatomi. During the same period as Tamah and Mr. Arnwine's marriage, white mobs burned and destroyed the "Black Wall Street" section of Tulsa, Oklahoma, not far from where they lived.

These American stories expanded my view from my Jewish perch, and I interpreted them in the ways I had learned from the stories in the ancient texts—stories both real and metaphoric.

As I read Aunt Rose and Mr. Arnwine's 1957 divorce decree, which stated that Mr. Arnwine had been found guilty of "several acts of extreme and repeated cruelty," my mind shifted to the brutal, heartless violence used to commandeer land in the Americas from Indigenous peoples. I saw the violence, from Oklahoma and Texas to Missouri and then Michigan, that was used to wrest the very land Aunt Rose and Mr. Arnwine were negotiating over during their divorce. Then my gaze shifted to Canaan and Jerusalem, and then to Israel and Palestine. The violence of conquering, of superiority, of racism repeating again and again.

Aunt Rose's brief obituary in the *Cassopolis Vigilant* revealed that she was a "former member of the Peoples Protestant

Church in Cassopolis," the nearby county seat. On the surface, this statement indicated that Aunt Rose may have become a Christian after moving to Cass County.

My first reaction to reading her obituary was denial; I latched onto the word "former" in the description of her church membership. She was buried in a church cemetery, but I had not considered that as evidence of her faith. When my mother spent over a decade in a nursing home where she was the only Jew, she attended all the Christian religious services; she enjoyed the singing and the company.

When my Aunt Rose moved with her African American husband to Cass County, her Jewish family cut ties with her, and at the same time she lived among people whose faith in God infused all aspects of their lives. I didn't know whether Aunt Rose was like my mother, finding community—but not a new faith—in Christian prayer and song.

When I think of Aunt Rose, I know I'm holding onto my doubts because conversion to Christianity brings up complicated emotions. Christian equals not Jewish; this has been a categorical truth in my life. But categorical truths are not beyond examination.

A fact of my life that may be familiar to other Jews, and I expect will surprise many Christians, is that just the sight of a cross triggers a fight-or-flight response in me. Rushing hormones from my brain spread to every part of my body. My body seems to feel the imprint of centuries of forced and violent conversions my ancestors experienced under the threat of death or expulsion. My younger daughter seems to feel this every time she sees a county sheriff's car.

My older daughter wears a delicate, golden cross necklace. For her, I think, the cross is a symbol of Jesus's protective love and her submission to the word of God. Of course, I don't want to fight or flee when I see my daughter. I want to open my heart further, meaning I have to explore my instinctive reactions, my experiences with Christianity, and the elements of my own identity and faith. I need to look at how I feel about a Jew who grew up in a Jewish family—like my daughter and Aunt Rose—praying to God in Jesus's name. For my daughter, I know her relationships with Christian African Americans were portals into her spiritual journey to God. And my daughter still says she is Jewish. She can neither discount her upbringing nor her encounters with God through Jesus.

Although I had hoped to help my daughters find community with other Jews of color through attending the yearly retreat of the Jewish Multiracial Network, as my older daughter has said, "Traveling two thousand miles to spend time with other Jews of color wasn't fulfilling" in terms of community. The "open tent" of Judaism, which expresses an intention that Jews of all persuasions are welcome in the kahal/community, without regard to politics or adherence to halacha (Jewish religious law), never quite felt like a home for her. She became bat mitzvah, joined a Jewish choir, was a teaching assistant at synagogue school, and went to Israel with other ninth graders, yet she never had a spiritually fulfilling experience.

She discovered that, for many of her Black friends, sustenance and safety came directly from God and were experienced through a direct relationship with Jesus. Her Jewish experiences offered neither community nor the connection with God she found in Christianity. Through Christianity, though, she has learned to recognize Jesus as a Jew.

Over the course of my writing this book about my Aunt Rose and trying to understand what being a member of the Peoples Protestant Church might have meant to Aunt Rose, my older daughter has become reborn and saved. She is ecstatic that she can talk to God directly, that she has found a safe harbor, that God is revealing her life's purpose, and that she has found a spiritual community in which to grow in her faith. Although we talk often about how God has entered her life, I am just beginning to understand and try to put into words her experience of God transforming her life.

When my older daughter and I speak openly, I hear her learning to read scripture in personally impactful ways, and when I study scripture with her, I have opportunities to examine my own beliefs. Jewish religious and spiritual practice has boundaries, but through learning about her way of relating to God, my teaching/learning of Jewish prayer and my relationship to God has gathered *koach* (strength).

When my daughters were young, many Jews asked me if I intended to raise them Jewish. At the time, I relegated this question to the category of inconsiderate and intrusive questions foisted on families with adopted children. On top of that, unbridled curiosity seems to dominate all other considerations when white people see interracial families. Jewish questioners, ignorant of their racial assumptions, were confused or perhaps just curious about how I would raise Black children as Jews. I often answered the question with a slightly huffy, "How else can a Jew raise their children?" But I then added, "When they are adults, of course, they will choose their own spiritual paths." Still, the question interjected doubt and acted as a wedge, undermining my confidence in my parenting and ability to transfer the gift of Jewishness to my daughters.

My relationship to Judaism is idiosyncratic and is more about my relationships with people and history than my belief in God. I've lived this Jewishness of mine with a high degree of unconscious security (and bias) in knowing that my genetic family has been Ashkenazi Jewish for as far back as can be traced. When I taught kids in Jewish religious school, I would ask them to imagine holding hands with a chain of one hundred people, each representing a generation beginning with their parents, grandparents, great-grandparents, and so on. In this way, we could imagine holding hands in a chain that reached backward to biblical Hebrews (well, not quite, but it was the idea). The Jewish students came to see that they were links in a real-life chain.

But this physical metaphor was insufficient for my own daughters and is an example of how my thinking about my Jewish identity limited its transferability to them. My loving them, in the words of Audre Lorde, made them "of my people," and reflexively changes who "my" people are.

When I was growing up in the white suburbs of St. Louis, Missouri, our family's social circle was completely Jewish. When I was seven years old (in 1962) and Black families had started moving into our near-to-the-city neighborhood, my family joined the flight to a solidly white suburb farther west. In this newly built subdivision in an unincorporated area near Creve Coeur, about half the families were Jewish, and I knew each one. Some had lived on the same blocks as my father when he was a kid. My parents refused proximity with African Americans, but they also ran toward something: the safety of a Jewish community.

I don't remember ever having non-Jews as guests in our home. It was an unstated norm. But our separation from

African Americans was different. While several Black men worked for my father in his used machinery business and Black women occasionally cleaned our house, my father instructed my siblings and me to never bring a Black friend into our home. My father's racism stunned me, drove an unbreachable wedge between us, and influenced me in ways I still struggle to unravel. Its bitterness mystified me, which in turn created a coldhearted edge to my feelings toward him and the racism that he embraced.

My father was certainly not alone in enforcing strict racial segregation. He was among the majority of white Americans. If they wanted to, every white person in America could describe, as I have begun to do, a thousand situations in which anti-Black racism has been perpetrated by their white friends, family, and selves.

I want to reach through time and put my arm around Aunt Rose. I want my twenty-year-old self and her sixty-eight-year-old self to hold hands at my father's funeral and regret, together, what was lost because of the scourge of racism. I want Aunt Rose to embrace me, both of us bending under the knowledge of racism's distortion within our families and communities. I wish I could hold Aunt Rose and share our regrets, yet regret is not the point of these stories.

This story attaches my link in *di goldene keyt* (the golden chain) of Jewish life to Aunt Rose's link and to my father's. I want to do the work my father could not—to include Aunt Rose and Zebedee Arnwine into the family I love. We Jews do that by telling stories. Telling the stories over and over—looking for meaning—is the way of our people.

ACKNOWLEDGMENTS

The descendants of Gracie and Albartis Arnwine are numerous and spread across the earth. Some of them are seeking to reclaim the land that was willed to them in 1855 and then hastily stolen. In writing this story of my Aunt Rose and Zebedee Arnwine, I did not want to exploit the Arnwines' story for my own satisfaction and gain. After all, as I write in the introduction, a people's stories belong to them as a source and form of cultural wealth. Even when our stories touch and overlap, a family's stories are personal and particular to them.

Early on, I found the Arnwine family's Facebook page, and through that, Candice Hammons, who is working to recover the land that was stolen from the Arnwines. In the 2023 book *Truth and Justice for the Arnwine Family*, Candice Hammons and Mary Tucker compile the stories of the Arnwine family and the theft of their inheritance. I hope you will offer support to the Arnwine Family Project by visiting https://www.change.org/Justice4theArnwineFamily and Candice's website, https://candicehammons.com/.

• • •

When you publish your first book at age seventy, how do you begin to acknowledge all the people who've gotten you to this point? The first people to see any of my early work on this book were members of my writing group in Ann Arbor, Michigan: Jill Halpern, Dawn Richberg, and my wife Patti. Without their encouragement, I wouldn't have gone beyond the first four pages that I tentatively wrote in 2016.

My most constant readers were my wife Patti, my sister Sheila Fisher, and my friends Ellen Rifkin and Irena Klepfisz. They read and critiqued more drafts of every section than could possibly be counted.

I sent drafts to anyone who said they'd take a look, but only some actually read them and sent me encouragement and substantive comments. I am grateful to each: Sarah Jacobus, Ellen Cassedy, Larry Bush, Marla Brettschneider, Rita Falbel, Tova Stabin, Dan Shenk, Laura Levitt, Lea Kosnik, Richard Weiss, Susan York, Rabbi Ora Nitkin-Kaner, Sharon Simeon, Ellie DesPrez, and Susan Steinhorn Lowry (and her mother, Marcia Steinhorn *z'l*, whose pointed "What's the point?" comments forced me to continually examine why I needed to tell these stories). If you gave me feedback on my manuscript but I have failed to mention you here, please forgive me and know that I listened to and read every bit of feedback I received and am grateful.

My Ann Arbor Reconstructionist Congregation *mishpokhe* group, Debbie Field, Hannah Davis, Kate Levin, Gillian Jackson, SallyGeorge Wright, Laurie White, Etta Heisler, Idelle Hammond-Sass, and Janet Greenhut, listened to me talk about the manuscript for years. I am very grateful for their support.

In 2019, when I was deep into the writing, I became publisher and editor of the *Washtenaw Jewish News*, a monthly print newspaper. I knew I needed to synergize if I was going to both finish the book and publish the newspaper, so I gave myself the opportunity and commitment to publish 1,500 words of the developing book each month in the newspaper. I did this for twenty-six months under the title "Looking for Rose." I wrote much of the book in these monthly installments. The Washtenaw Jewish community was an encouraging first audience, and I hope they know how grateful I am to them.

I couldn't have told this story without the support, knowledge, and care of Marshall H. Sanders Jr. and Sharon Simeon. Marshall and Sharon are the unexpected and cherished gifts of this whole project. Others from Vandalia who helped me with crucial information and perspective were Sally Connor and Ruth Anderson Walker.

My cousins Laura Dusseau and David Asher sent me invaluable photos of my father's family.

Jeannette Gabriel shared important research about interracial organizing in Muskogee, Oklahoma, and St. Louis, Missouri.

Laura Cohen spent time in the State Historical Society of Missouri at the University of Missouri–St. Louis for me and helped me locate some of the images in this book.

When I thought I was almost done, Enoch Page critiqued a draft with both encouragement and necessary corrections on how to include insights from my daughters without exploiting them.

Lana Povitz pointed me toward Wayne State University Press and their acquisitions editor Sandra Korn, whose enthusiasm for this book helped me get past the "it's almost done" stage.

I wrote most of this book while our younger daughter was in high school and the older one was in college. Perhaps less physically challenging parenting years but certainly not less challenging. For much of the time, my computer and desk were in the middle of the living room, next to the kitchen. I carved out time when I was alone and when people were around. My beautiful family tolerated it all with no complaints (about my writing, anyway). I've mentioned Patti above as a reader (and her critiques were invaluable), but I have to express here my gratitude for her and our daughters' unflagging support through the whole process. I love you all more than I can ever express.

BIBLIOGRAPHY

Azoulay, Katya Gibel. *Black, Jewish, and Interracial: It's Not the Color of Your Skin, but the Race of Your Kin, and Other Myths of Identity*. Duke University Press, 1997.

Born in Slavery: Slave Narratives from the Federal Writers' Project, 1936 to 1938. Manuscript Division, Library of Congress, and Prints and Photographs Division, Library of Congress, 2001.

Cherokee County Historical Commission (Texas). *Cherokee County History*. Jacksonville, Texas: University of North Texas Libraries, the Portal to Texas History, 2001. https://texashistory.unt.edu/ark:/67531/metapth354360/.

Cox, Anna-Lisa. *A Stronger Kinship: One Town's Extraordinary Story of Hope and Faith*. University of Nebraska Press, 2007.

Culiner, Jill. *Finding Home: In the Footsteps of the Jewish Fusgeyers*. Sumach Press, 2004.

Drake, St. Clair, and Horace R. Cayton. *Black Metropolis: A Study of Negro Life in a Northern City*. Revised and enlarged edition. University of Chicago Press, 1993.

Eldridge, Carrie. *Cabell County's Empire for Freedom: The Manumission of Sampson Sander's Slaves*. John Deaver Drinko Academy for American Political Institution and Civic Culture, Marshall University, 1999.

Feurer, Rosemary. *Radical Unionism in the Midwest, 1900–1950.* University of Illinois Press, 2006.

Franklin, John Hope, and John Whittington Franklin, eds. *My Life and an Era: The Autobiography of Buck Colbert Franklin.* Louisiana State University Press, 1997.

Grant, Gail Milissa. *At the Elbows of My Elders: One Family's Journey Toward Civil Rights.* Missouri History Museum: Distributed by the University of Missouri Press, 2008.

Hesslink, George K. *Black Neighbors: Negroes in a Northern Rural Community.* Bobbs-Merrill, 1968.

Johnson, Hannibal B. *Acres of Aspiration: The All-Black Towns in Oklahoma.* Eakin Press, 2002.

Loewen, James W. *Sundown Towns: A Hidden Dimension of American Racism.* New Press, 2018.

McKissack, Patricia C., and Fredrick L. McKissack. *Young, Black, and Determined: A Biography of Lorraine Hansberry.* Holiday House, 1998.

Painter, Nell Irvin. *Exodusters: Black Migration to Kansas After Reconstruction.* University Press of Kansas, 1986.

Perry, Imani. *Looking for Lorraine: The Radiant and Radical Life of Lorraine Hansberry.* Beacon Press, 2018.

Plaskow, Judith, and Donna Berman. *The Coming of Lilith: Essays on Feminism, Judaism, and Sexual Ethics, 1972–2003.* Beacon Press, 2005.

Sawyer, Marcia Renee. "Surviving Freedom: African American Farm Households in Cass County, Michigan, 1832–1880." PhD diss., Michigan State University, 1991. ProQuest (9134163).

Steinberg, Bernard. "Moses Maimonides: *Mishneh* Torah." In *Oxford Bibliographies.* Modified May 24, 2017. Accessed January 31, 2023. http://www.oxfordbibliographies.com/view/document/obo-9780199840731/obo-9780199840731-0152.xml.

Stephens, Ronald Jemal. *Idlewild: The Rise, Decline, and Rebirth of a Unique African American Resort Town.* University of Michigan Press, 2013.

Wimbush, Vincent L., and Rosamond C. Rodman. *African Americans and the Bible: Sacred Texts and Social Textures*. Continuum, 2000.

Yerushalmi, Yosef Hayim. *Zakhor: Jewish History and Jewish Memory*. University of Washington Press, 1996.

Zipperstein, Steven J. *Pogrom: Kishinev and the Tilt of History*. Liveright Publishing Corporation, 2018.

ABOUT THE AUTHOR

CLARE KINBERG is the publisher and editor of the *Washtenaw Jewish News*, a monthly newspaper in southeast Michigan, and was the editor of the international literary/political biannual *Bridges: A Jewish Feminist Journal* from 1989 to 2011. For many years, she worked as a librarian and teacher and as director of religious schools in various Jewish denominations. Kinberg has been an organizer in the lesbian, feminist, and anti-war movements for more than forty years. Her writing on Jewish culture, the Jewish Labor Bund, and Israel/Palestine has appeared in *Tablet*, *Sh'ma*, *Bridges*, *Detroit Jewish News*, and many other publications.